W9-BNU-912

what the dog did

what the dog did

*tales from a formerly
reluctant dog owner*

emily yoffe

BLOOMSBURY

Published by Bloomsbury Publishing, New York and London
Distributed to the trade by Holtzbrinck Publishers

All papers used by Bloomsbury Publishing are natural, recyclable products made
from wood grown in well-managed forests. The manufacturing processes
conform to the environmental regulations of the country of origin.

Library of Congress Cataloging-in-Publication Data

Yoffe, Emily.
    What the dog did : tales from a formerly reluctant dog owner / Emily Yoffe.
    p. cm.
    ISBN 1-58234-564-3 (hardcover)
    ISBN-13 978-1-58234-564-2
1. Dogs—United States—Anecdotes. 2. Yoffe, Emily. I. Title.

SF426.2.Y64 2005
636.7'0887—dc22

2004023840

Portions of this book originally appeared, in different form, on Slate.com.

Author's note: Out of concern for the privacy of others,
some names have been changed and identities disguised.

First U.S. Edition 2005

1 3 5 7 9 10 8 6 4 2

Typeset by Palimpsest Book Production Limited,
Polmont, Stirlingshire, Scotland
Printed in the United States of America
by Quebecor World Fairfield

CONTENTS

To my husband and daughter

INTRODUCTION

The lowest point in my transformation into a dog person came one drizzly night at eleven P.M., three months after we got our beagle, Sasha. I used to laugh at dog owners when I drove home on late, wet nights, seeing them standing like demented courtiers holding umbrellas over their dogs. Now here I was, sodden and tired, waiting for Sasha to relieve herself.

After she squatted repeatedly without effect and with apparent distress, I finally bent down to check out the problem. Illuminated by the streetlight, I saw something white and stringy hanging out her rear end. As if slipping on a surgical glove, I stuck my hand into one of the plastic newspaper bags that now always fashionably bulged out of my pockets. My chance to practice medicine without a license, I thought as I grabbed the object and yanked. It was long and stretchy, with a metal circle on one end, and when I finally confiscated all of it—to Sasha's ecstasy—I realized I'd seen it before. It was the strap of my favorite bra. The bra had vanished a few days earlier; both my husband and daughter denied any knowledge of its whereabouts. (If my husband had stolen it, did I really want to know?)

"You're no longer a suspect," I said to him when I returned. "Sasha ate my bra."

"That shows how much she loves you," he said wanly. Since he was responsible for our becoming a dog-owning family, he was always trying to convince me how my life had changed for the better.

"How much do you love me?" I asked, thinking of which undergarments he could ingest to prove it. Our conversation was interrupted by the sound of Sasha tipping over the kitchen garbage can.

Many Buddhists believe that for a human to be reincarnated as a dog is punishment for being rotten in your past life. I am no expert in comparative religion, but I felt this conviction may have gotten things backward. It seemed more likely that as the baby boom was taking off a naughty dog died and came back as me. How else to explain the karma of being a middle-aged cat person whose life was now devoted to the care, feeding, training, and rectal maintenance of a formerly stray beagle?

How much of a cat person was I? During the hundred or so years I was single, my clothing was so covered with cat hair that I was afraid anti-fur activists would dump cans of paint on me. I spent hours baby-talking to my cats. Once as I was scooping the litter box, I heard through the heat pipe in the apartment bathroom my downstairs neighbor call to her husband, "Are you proud of my big poopie?" using exactly the same syntax and singsong cadence with which I praised my cats' daily functions.

Going from cat owner to dog owner made me realize that cats are private, dogs are public. To know your cat someone has to be invited into your domain. But when you have a dog, there it is on the end of your arm like an accessory, a statement about your self-image. I've always been told that my normal expression is one of grimness, my failed attempt at looking sophisticated and detached. But it's impossible to be grim, or sophisticated, or detached, with a floppy-eared beagle pulling you along the street. Actually, when you're walking your dog, you're simply the means by which the dog presents herself to the world.

Sasha is lucky she's beautiful. Superficial as it is, it's hard to stay mad at such a gorgeous creature. Walking her has given me a glimpse of what it must be like to be married to a celebrity. People stop their cars and call out, "She's so cute!" Couples walking past will smile and nudge each other, making sure they each see her. Children stop and say, "Can I touch her?" Middle-aged people bend down to her and inevitably say, "A beagle! I had a beagle when I was a kid." (This makes me wonder if a message went out to everyone else about thirty years ago: "Don't get another beagle.")

She is small, only thirteen inches high at the shoulder and sixteen pounds. Because of her size, she has the look of a perpetual puppy. Nefertiti would be jealous of her huge, kohl-rimmed eyes. Her head is fawn-colored, stippling to black at her neck. Her ears are silky and honey brown. On her neck is a lightning-shaped blaze of white (we gave her Lightning as a middle name). Her back is rich black, her belly and tip of her tail white.

Walking a dog was a revelation. Who knew so many of my neighbors, most of whom I'd never seen before, owned dogs? It was like finding out that, at some nightly prearranged signal, people all around me were sneaking out to go ballroom dancing or form covens. I learned the strange etiquette of dog ownership: We don't introduce ourselves, just our dogs. So Sasha knows Tasha and Pasha (I'm not kidding), but I have no idea who their owners are.

After I got Sasha, the owner of Harry, the aged, decrepit

schnauzer down the street, stopped me one day. Harry's Owner and I talked for the first time in eight years of being neighbors. Harry's Owner congratulated me on Sasha and said with the deepest gravity, "You will experience such joy." As he spoke Harry looked at me with rheumy eyes, his muzzle caked with dried dog food. Harry lifted his leg and urine dribbled down the stained fur. "Good boy," Harry's Owner said tenderly. I remembered visiting nursing homes and seeing relatives in such condition—their senses going, unable to clean themselves, incontinent. "Joy" was not my primary emotion. But Sasha is young and vital, so I knew I would experience the joy, the lowered blood pressure, the reduction in stress hormones that you are told is a reward of dog ownership.

I'm glad, however, that I didn't have on a blood pressure cuff the day I saw Sasha emerge from the basement—the territory of the cats—licking kitty-litter pellets from her snout. It wasn't the equivalent of discovering a crack pipe in my child's underwear drawer, but it was disheartening to realize my dog considered cat feces an *amuse-bouche*. Nor did my diastolic reading take a dive the day, while walking Sasha down the block, I noticed she had something in her mouth and was vigorously chewing on it. I bent down, pried her jaws open, and extracted a used condom. This made me worry not only about dog ownership, but about my neighbors.

Dogs have evolved to be scavengers, experts say. But dogs aren't just scavengers, they're indiscriminate scavengers. How is it that a species could be so successful, yet not know it's a bad idea to eat condoms?

After I told some friends about Sasha's desire to make me wear strapless bras, one said I had to talk to his sister. I called Clarissa who told me that her two-year-old Labrador retriever, Marley, had a passion for baked goods. Knowing this, Clarissa figured out just how far Marley's reach extended at every point in her kitchen.

One Sunday morning she was baking bread. While the dough was rising in a glass bowl, she pushed it to the back of the stove, and left to run some errands. When she returned the bowl and the dough were no longer on the stove. On the floor was shattered glass, a few small lumps of dough, and blood. Clarissa located Marley hiding behind a couch, her face cut and bloody. She had eaten the dough off the floor, broken glass and all.

Since it was Sunday (Sunday is dogs' preferred day of the week for deadly ingestion) she took Marley to the emergency animal hospital, where Clarissa told the receptionist her dog had eaten a pile of glass. As she sat in the waiting room, Marley draped over her lap, she noticed that her dog's midsection appeared to be expanding. Marley let out a thunderous belch and the room was filled with the enticing aroma of baking bread. Marley was rising! The belching and the baking continued until the vet showed up to take Marley off for an X-ray. Marley's problem was not glass—she hadn't eaten much—but dough. Because of the warmth of Marley's stomach, the bread was going to rise until it exploded. Marley went in for surgery to have, at a cost of $3,000, the world's most expensive loaf of bread removed.

My bra story reminded someone else of a malamute who made Sasha look like a picky eater. It turned out that as a year-old puppy Tina, already seventy-five pounds, was kept in the kitchen during the day while her owner, Karl, was at work. Even a malamute can't do that much damage to major appliances, he figured. This appeared to be true until he came home one day, walked and fed Tina, and went to the refrigerator to start dinner. When he opened the door he discovered the gasket—the rubber tubing that keeps the refrigerator door sealed—was missing. All of it. Had Tina hidden it? A search turned up nothing. It was hard to believe she had been able to eat such an impressive tube of rubber, but if she had, it wasn't bothering her.

The next morning Karl took Tina for her walk, and she ended the mystery. It took Karl about five minutes of pulling to unspool from Tina the entire, intact, many-feet-long gasket, which he described as being "like a large piece of dental floss." While one mystery ended, another has never been solved: How did she keep it in one piece? It was lucky she did. Instead of a $3,000 vet bill for gasket removal, Karl had only a $200 repair bill for gasket replacement.

When you have a dog, crazy stuff happens. I started clipping newspaper stories about just how crazy. There was the one about the bull terrier puppy in Liverpool whose owner noticed that he didn't curl up to sleep anymore. It turns out the puppy had swallowed a seven-inch knife—plastic end first—that was the length of his body. He recovered completely from his surgical cutlery excision.

Then there was the hunter in South Dakota who got shot by his English setter. After bagging seven pheasants the hunter lined them up for a photograph, leaving his twelve-gauge shotgun nearby. His year-old hunting dog, prancing around, stepped on the gun, discharging the pellets into the hunter's ankle. His ankle was patched up. I imagined, however, after your dog shoots you your dignity suffers a fatal blow. I thought I had found the only shot-by-your-dog story. But a few months later I read an article about a man in Florida who decided the best way to get rid of a litter of unwanted three-month-old puppies was to shoot them. While he was holding two of the doomed puppies, one pressed its paw on the trigger, causing a bullet to go through the man's wrist. I realized then that guns don't injure people, puppies with guns injure people.

Early in my life with Sasha I wrote a piece for Slate.com about the shock of dog ownership. I expected to be denounced, but I was overwhelmed with e-mails of encouragement. This confirmed my impression that dog owners are among the nicest group of people I'd ever encountered. Or at least when you encounter people with their dog, they tend to be nice. Since dogs force you into social situations, even owners who aren't naturally gregarious are obliged to be sociable. I even know two married couples who met because they were first attracted to each other's dogs. This doesn't happen with cats. During my dating years my cats were less an enticement than a screening device. Potential suitors' reactions ranged from hostility to indifference.

Even I was becoming friendlier because of Sasha. One day, while visiting Manhattan, I stopped two men—both dressed in black leather and covered in body piercings and tattoos—who were walking a beagle. I told them I had a beagle at home, and we immediately bonded over our shared experience of urban beagle life.

The Slate readers promised me life with a dog would get better, and it has (or else I've simply forgotten what life was like before Sasha). They also sent many "I can top that" anecdotes. Like the one about the puppy who by his first birthday had punctured a lung, been rescued from drowning in the goldfish pond, and had stomach surgery to remove a swallowed rock.

I realized almost everyone I knew with a dog had a story. Maybe companionship and someone to lick your feet isn't what really motivates people to have dogs. Maybe being able to tell dog stories is. A friend told me she had a friend who went through an unusual burial ritual each time one of his dogs died. So I called Michael, who explained that he and his adult siblings feel that a dog is not at peace unless it is interred in the family's informal pet burial ground at their childhood home in Milwaukee. This has sometimes required long-term planning. Michael, who owned a ski lodge in Colorado, said one of his most recent dogs, Windsor, was a too-clever Welsh terrier who was constantly getting into trouble. He was an escape artist who could be found on top of ladders, or taking off down the road. He was destined to be hit by a car, and when he was, Michael decided although Windsor had never been to Milwaukee, it had to be his final resting place.

The problem was that it was the height of ski season and the lodge was fully booked. There was an obvious interim solution: Michael stuck Windsor in a snowbank. When spring came, before Windsor started to thaw, Michael moved him to the freezer in the kitchen, which fortunately was off-limits to guests. Finally, the guests thinned out and Michael booked a plane to Wisconsin. Windsor seemed solid, so Michael got a picnic cooler, put the late terrier inside, and checked him through as luggage. All was fine until Michael stood at baggage claim. As the cooler came off the belt, several suitcases smashed into it, causing the top to come off, and Windsor, still icy, to pop out. Michael kept his cool, replaced his dog and the cooler top, and without making eye contact with the rest of the passengers, left the airport. Windsor now has a special place by the stream out back.

As I started collecting dog stories, I was stunned by how many friends I had whose dog had saved a life. And how many whose dogs' eating and regurgitation rituals had required them to redecorate the house.

I discovered that it wasn't always the dog's fault that previously important components of one's existence—family, work, running a home, sleep—became subordinate to the needs of the dog. I was talking to a dog owner who told me how his Dutch shepherd drove him and his wife crazy with a wake-up routine that started at five-thirty A.M. The dog, Riley, ran an ever-faster circuit around the bed, panting loudly, then bumping the mattress. When I asked how Riley was able to get all the way around the bed, his owner explained that the bed was pulled out from the wall.

"Why?" I asked.

"Because Riley likes to run around it."

This book is also an account of my unexpected journey to becoming a dog person. How else can I explain how I ended up being the foster mother to a series of homeless beagles? Not that I don't still love cats. As Winston Churchill said, "Dogs look up to you, cats look down on you." It's just that I discovered that being looked at from both those perspectives is where I want to be.

1

"DOGS ARE WHO I AM"

How getting a dog had to be preferable to my family's whining about not having one.

When my daughter was born, I still had the pair of cats I'd gotten as kittens when I was twenty-five. But Shlomo died of cancer at age sixteen. She had always slept by my head, her purr lulling me like an electronic sleep aid sold in catalogues. My other cat, Sabra, lasted another five years. In her final months she was curled in a ball on a chair in the den. Since she had gold and black stripes, it was like having a coonskin cap for a pet that recoiled if you touched it. Wanting my daughter to have lively companions, I found a newspaper ad for a pair of kitten brothers rescued from—what else?—the home of an old lady with seventy-five cats. Of course they were fluffy and blond, the better to decorate my black pants for the next twenty years. My daughter named them Goldie and Biscuit. I thought I had our pet situation set.

Shortly after the kittens' arrival, my preliterate daughter managed to write her first sentence: "I love dogs." Then she came home from kindergarten with a chart of everyone's favorite pet—

hers was dog. When I mentioned she had cats, not a dog, she said, "They asked for my favorite, not what I have."

She cut out dog pictures and taped them all over her room. Her most frequently borrowed library book was an enormous American Kennel Club guide to dog breeds. Instead of bedtime stories, she wanted to look through the book, deciding what kind of dog she'd get when she was old enough to leave home. "When I'm in college I'm going to have my own dog and you can't do anything about it," she said. I began to dread visiting friends who had dogs. My daughter would get down on the floor and commune with them, paws and arms wrapped around each other. When I had to disentangle her, days of mourning over her dogless state ensued.

I sometimes wonder about Sasha's fate, and mine, if we hadn't gone to brunch at my friend Jane's a week after the arrival of their yellow Labrador puppy, Dugan. My six-year-old daughter spent the whole morning clinging to its mushy body and stroking its floppy ears. When we left she collapsed. "I don't have anything I want! I don't have a brother. I don't have a sister. I don't have a dog. Dogs are who I am. Dogs are my life."

My husband was so moved by her self-understanding that he started in on me. "She is crying out to us about what she needs," he said.

"I am crying out to you about what I don't need," I said. "Who will walk the dog? Me! Who will take the dog to the vet? Me! Who will make dog-sitting arrangements on the rare occasion I leave my home office like some defiant Taliban wife? Me!"

"Listen to your daughter. She wants something to love. She doesn't even have siblings."

My husband knew exactly how old I was when he married me. The fact that all I had left in my fallopian tubes was the equivalent of the Chinese delicacy thousand-year-old eggs was an unfair argument for getting a dog.

So how did I become a dog owner? My husband and daughter finally ground me down in one of those emotional assaults that are usually characterized as "family life."

I agreed to research an appropriate breed for our family ("Who will do all the work of finding a dog? Me!"). What is it with breeds? When you have cats occasionally you get asked, "What kind of cat do you have?" I always answer "Indoors." Sure, I know there's a difference between a Siamese and a Maine coon, but most cats are generic. Go to the zoo and look at the cat house—lions, tigers, caracals, jaguarundi—they're all variations on the same template. But dogs! Across the street from me is a family that owns a Great Dane and another that owns a miniature dachshund. The Great Dane would look normal only if being walked by Sasquatch; the miniature dachshund you could lay in front of your computer keyboard and use as a wrist rest. Yet these two creatures are both dogs—they could even mate and produce something you don't want to think about.

What is it with breeders? Each breed is supposed to match a "standard," which makes me think that the dog-breeding world is made up of people who were laughed at in high school for having hairy moles or buckteeth, and are now getting even by setting ridiculous rules for dogs' appearance. Who cares that the ridge on a Rhodesian ridgeback's back has an extra whorl? Or that an affenpinscher's expression is insufficiently monkeylike? Why are there no standards for the handlers who run dogs around the show ring? Lush acrylic toupees, and pendulous, flapping breasts don't get them disqualified.

When you look at some of the work breeders do, it makes you think these people should have been forced to get another hobby, like sniffing airplane glue, that affects only their DNA, not another creature's. Who thought it would be a good idea to require bulldogs to have such huge skulls that giving birth to these King

Kong–headed puppies will kill the mother unless delivered by cesarean section? Or take the Chinese crested—this is a hairless dog with puffs of fur ringing the feet that makes it look as if it's wearing a marabou-feathered peignoir. You get the feeling dogs like this are bred just to prove it could be done.

As I surveyed the information about various breeds it occurred to me that the dirty secret of dog lovers is that they enjoy the fact that every breed is impossible. How else to explain site after site, created by the breed's fanciers no less, that described them variously as "excitable," "hard to train," "massive shedder," "needing constant attention," "not good with children," "strong destructive impulse." My family rejected my findings that in the twelve or so millennia since dogs were domesticated none has been developed that met our needs.

Finally, I settled on the perfect breed for us—the Boston terrier. It's small, odorless, agreeable, short-coated, devoted, easy to train, and its nickname is "The American Gentleman." Since I'm from Boston, the little black-and-white dog struck a nostalgic chord with me. I even came up with a name: Bosco, after the chocolate syrup I poured into milk as a child. Looking at Boston terrier sites, I saw that breeders had done it no favors. Since the early twentieth century, they had been producing dogs with increasingly short muzzles and bug eyes. I was hoping we could find a less extreme throwback.

When I told my sister that to stop the nightly harassment I was considering getting a Boston terrier, she said, "It's in your genes!"

"I don't have bug eyes," I replied.

"No, I mean Pup," she said, referring to our late grandfather. "He would be so proud."

"Why?" I asked.

"Come on. Aren't you interested in Boston terriers because of Pup?"

"What are you talking about?"

"You didn't know? Pup bred Boston terriers when he was a young man. I have a picture of him with one."

I'd never seen the photo. I come from an unsentimental family where most memorabilia is stuffed in drawers. I was genetically programmed to have a Boston terrier! Not only that, my grandfather, who was born in Boston in 1898, might have had a hand in forming Boston terriers. I was starting to feel dog fate calling me.

I e-mailed a few Boston terrier sites to my husband at work. He quickly called. "They all look like Marty Feldman," he complained, referring to the late film comedian with wild walleyes.

"I thought you liked Marty Feldman," I said.

"I did. But I never wanted to take him for walks."

"I'll walk Marty."

That afternoon I showed my daughter the Web sites. "Look, this is the kind of dog we might get," I said, expecting a hug.

"If that dog was in my room when I went to bed I would never sleep for the rest of my life," she said.

I explained that if I was going to cave in and get a dog, then this was the breed we were going to get. My daughter burst into tears. "They scare me. Their eyes scare me!"

That night, when she ran to my husband crying about the mutant I was about to inflict on the family, my husband said, "We're doing this for her. You can't get a dog that terrifies her." Good-bye, Bosco.

I gave up on breeds altogether. I didn't want to support the breeding industry anyway. If we were going to get a dog, we'd do a good deed and save some mutt from the pound. I started looking at the Web sites of local rescue organizations. I discovered most of the people in this worthy business are dogists. They despise humans because humans neglect and abandon dogs. They believe all dogs are superior to all *Homo sapiens*, except those

Homo sapiens who share their view of canine superiority. Want proof? Here is part of a posting I found for a miniature pinscher named Adam. "Adam was 'rescued' from a back yard breeder that continued to breed until 'she' (the breeder) died THANKFULLY."

It became clear the descriptions of the dogs had to be read with an eye for euphemism. For example, "understands house-training." I understand marathon training; that doesn't mean I can run a marathon. "Best with families with no young children." That means surgeons were able to successfully reattach little Timmy's arm.

Other personal ads take a challenging tone, implying that you are a superficial jerk for rejecting this dog. "Humbert has three legs. You don't think that's enough legs? Well, look down and tell me how many legs you have." "Daisy Mae is a wonderful eleven-year-old girl who's still going strong. Her only sign of age is that she needs to be fed liquid formula through a turkey baster. She would be a great addition to a family where at least one person is home most of the day to give her the attention she deserves."

We entered the next phase, visiting animal shelters to look at actual dogs. Going to an animal shelter with a six-year-old is an excellent exercise if you like driving home from an animal shelter with a six-year-old sobbing, "Why couldn't we get Punkin?" Talk about guilt. The shelters let you take out of its cell any dog that catches your eye. You and the dog go to a special visitation room where you decide either you'll put in an application and save its life, or it's not for you and you'd like to sentence it to almost certain death. I felt cruel when I ruled out any dog that immediately urinated on me, or had more scabs than fur.

Then we encountered our first beagle, a sweet, tiny creature named Rosie who had been found wandering. The volunteer brought her out and we each held the little dog while she looked at us pleadingly. My daughter and Rosie went running together. I asked the volunteer about the problems I'd read about beagles on the various I-Live-for-Beagles Web sites: hard to housebreak, difficult to train, prone to run away, incessant baying. "I have a beagle, and none of that's true," she said. My daughter bent down to pet Rosie and said, "Don't worry, girl, you don't have to stay here." Rosie licked her face, and my daughter laughed. At that moment it didn't matter that we had just replaced the dining room rug. We put in a request for Rosie, but warned my daughter as we drove away that Rosie's owner might come and take her back. He did, the next day. To stanch the tears, we promised my daughter we would find a dog just as adorable. Losing Rosie was so painful that my daughter would only refer to her as "Osie." "If I say Rosie, I start to cry," she explained.

Konrad Lorenz won a Nobel Prize for discovering imprinting—that some newborn animals will assume their parents are the first creatures they see. He convinced a flock of geese that he was their mother. Now we were imprinted. We weren't looking for a dog, we were looking for a beagle. Our shelter volunteer had told us if we didn't get Rosie we should go to the Web site of a local organization called Beagle Rescue Education and Welfare, or BREW.

Each day after school my daughter and I scoured the BREW Web site. I took notes on possible candidates, analyzing each adjective, judging the aesthetics of each coat. Six weeks after we met, my husband and I were engaged. It has worked out great, but I'm not sure I invested as much time judging his markings as I was our potential beagle's.

The BREW site was refreshingly honest. BREW emphasized that you cannot get a beagle if you want a dog you can take off its leash. Not being a dog person yet, I didn't understand the implications of this information. Since then it has become like one of those quirks you find charming in your beloved when you're dating—"Oh, it's so cute that you *always* get lost!"—that becomes a grinding annoyance in a marriage. In its entry on beagles, *The International Encyclopedia of Dogs* states: "It is essential that the breed is trained to come when called, as this can avert disaster should a potential 'hunting' situation arise." Excellent advice, and as useful as a child-rearing book declaring: "It is crucial to instruct your offspring to become as rich as Bill Gates, as this can avert disaster should a potential financial obligation arise." Sasha has made it clear that however much love and food we pour into her, if the front door is ajar for a millisecond, she will take off down the street without a farewell glance, on the scent trail of a decomposing possum, or a sewerline break.

BREW listed a number of warnings about beagle ownership. If you want a dog that is easy to train, lives to obey, is a snap to housebreak, doesn't mess up the house, enjoys jogging with you or playing Frisbee, then, they advised, don't get a beagle. Getting a beagle after this was like reading about a car model in *Consumer Reports*: "If you want an automobile that will start reliably, requires little maintenance, runs in all kinds of weather, and has a good safety record, then this model is not for you," and then running to the dealer to put down a deposit on an Osie.

Still, beagles are so adorable, and have such an ancient history. It's not known where the name beagle came from. *The International Encyclopedia of Dogs* says that in Old English, the word *begle* means "little." The National Beagle Club also offers that in Old French *be'geule* means "gape throat"—a reference to baying of hounds in hot pursuit. In the guidebook *Beagles* by Lucia Parent, she writes that it's possible the forerunners of the breed came to England with William the Conquerer. They became favorites of the British royal family. Hunters in the first Queen Elizabeth's court kept the tiny beagles of the day—the now mythological "pocket beagle"—in the pocket of their hunting clothes.

However, in the matter of dogs, as in so much else, the royal family is no role model. I noticed in news reports that Princess Anne's bull terriers run rather amok. First, the bull terrier Dotty bit two children. This, according to Reuters, resulted in Anne's being the first British royal to be convicted of a criminal offense in 350 years—indicating it's legally safer for royals to decapitate their spouses than keep bull terriers. Then when Anne was visiting her mother, the queen, another one of Anne's bull terriers, Florence, so brutally attacked one of the queen's beloved corgis that the corgi had to be put down. I wonder if Dr. Phil would make a house call to Buckingham Palace to straighten out this psychological mess. Then Florence, while supposedly relaxing at the Sandringham estate, went on a rampage and bit a maid on the leg. Clearly, the royal family should have stuck with beagles.

That was our plan, so off we went to BREW's adoption fair, nervous about passing their screening process, making us worthy of a previously rejected dog. The event was held at a mega pet store, and near the entrance BREW volunteers held leashes as more than a dozen beagles bayed, circled, and cowered. I came with a pile of dog photos and bios I had printed out from the BREW Web site. I felt like Donald Trump asking for private interviews with candidates for Miss Universe.

The director of BREW, the warm, efficient Laura Charles, looked over the papers and made a series of snap judgments. Sissy was too wild; Carter was too phlegmatic; Ariel was already taken; Petunia had heartworm. She suggested I simply look at the dogs milling about, wearing yellow BREW bandanas indicating they were available.

Being surrounded by a roomful of abandoned creatures made me think that given the right circumstances I'd adopt a warthog.

That is, as long as it didn't smell like the first cute beagle I approached whose aroma was reminiscent of a tuna sandwich left too long in the sun.

Then we saw Conchita. It's a classic Hollywood story: the last-minute reprieve from death row. The organization had found Conchita just hours before her scheduled euthanasia at a West Virginia pound. Nothing was known of her life except that it had started about eighteen months before. Her coat was dull and full of dandruff and her skeleton poked from underneath it. She seemed beyond terror. Her enormous chocolate eyes were set in a fixed, resigned gaze that seemed to say, "I know something even worse is coming."

Her wretchedness moved us, and Laura suggested we take her for a walk and see if we bonded. We took Conchita to a grassy median strip in the mall parking lot. She followed us with neither resistance nor enthusiasm. We sat down and stroked her without engendering a response. Since we knew nothing about dogs, we were encouraged that she wasn't wild or noisy. She was pathetic. We agreed we had to have her.

When we took her back to the store a BREW volunteer came up to me and said a family had just come in who had seen Conchita on the Web site and were very interested in her. They were veteran beagle adopters and so would have first dibs. Afraid of a Rosie replay, my husband took my daughter and Conchita and sneaked to the back of the store, hiding among the ferret products. I pretended I had lost track of my family and began wandering aimlessly. Finally the woman insisted we cough up Conchita. I got my husband and daughter off the ferret bed and told them we had to take our chances. As we handed over Conchita my daughter said, "Every time I find a dog I want somebody takes it," and her eyes filled with tears.

Minutes later the volunteer ran up to us. "They didn't like her!

They didn't like her!" she said of the experienced beagle family's reaction to Conchita. We took this as great news.

During the fair we picked up a lot of beagle-rescue lore. We were told most abandoned beagles are failed hunting dogs. This was a bit of propaganda that only added to their appeal—"Oh, she'd rather sit in your lap than track bunnies." They never mentioned the possibility that maybe a failed house pet turned up now and then.

We filled out an application and paid the adoption fee. We couldn't take Conchita with us—BREW first had to send a caseworker to our home to make sure we weren't running a vivisection factory in our basement. "Oh, one thing you should know," said Laura. "Your dog is going to be completely unhousebroken."

"Sure, that's fine. It's wonderful, actually," I said, still mindful that we hadn't been approved for dog ownership. I was not in a position to comment that I thought the point of getting a grown dog was that somebody else had taken care of this dirty work. A week later we passed inspection and went to the kennel where Conchita had been boarding to pick her up. She was Sasha now, renamed by my daughter in honor of a schoolmate.

Sasha had just been bathed, and her shiny, fluffy fur made her seem even sadder—like a homeless waif dressed up in a ballgown. She was impassive on the ride home and terrified when she got in the house. It was likely she had never been in a house before, given her bafflement when she first confronted our staircase. She was so confused and scared. She roamed aimlessly around the house, occasionally coming up to one of us to give us what I called her sideways eye—turning her head, and peeking at us using peripheral vision.

Her arrival brought back memories of when my husband and I brought our newborn daughter home from the hospital. We were thrilled to be a family. We had prepared ourselves by reading the books, talking to friends, and taking the bringing-home-a-newborn class at the hospital. Now here we were, with a baby and no idea what to do. We figured we couldn't go wrong just attending to the basics: eating and elimination. That seemed the right approach to Sasha, too. After all, even if people hadn't been taking care of dogs for as long as they'd been taking care of babies, it had been going on for about twelve thousand years. How hard could it be?

2

STARVED FOR AFFECTION

*The tortured history of my childhood
German shepherd, Brandy.*

Before I got Sasha, I had only lived with one other dog. We got him when I was ten following a burglary at our house. My parents decided an alarm system was too expensive and troublesome to maintain. A guard dog would be less work and also teach us valuable lessons in something or other. A few weeks later my parents drove up with a German shepherd puppy my mother named Brandy. My father walked the puppy into the yard, as my younger brother and sister and I jumped around him ecstatically. Then Brandy made an enormous bowel movement and the three of us decided to run inside and watch TV. My father yelled, "Hey, where do you think you're going? You think having a pet is five minutes of kitchy-koo? *This* is what having a pet is about," he said, pointing to the pile. We kept running. "Someone bring me a plastic bag!" he called as we reached the front door.

Those first minutes established the parameters of Brandy's life— neglect punctuated by bursts of affection. The birth of my youngest brother closely followed Brandy's arrival, so my overwhelmed parents had the same response to Brandy as they did to the rest of us: "You're hungry *again*?" His training consisted of, "You figure it out."

My parents had gotten a German shepherd because of the breed's reputation as fearsome watchdogs. Brandy ignited in my siblings and me a desire to see the next intruder reduced to a pulpy mass that we could prop in the front yard as a warning to the intruder after that. We went around the house opening windows in the dead of winter and unlocking the front door in hopes someone would tiptoe in to find himself given the meat-tenderizer treatment by Brandy's jaws.

But it soon became clear that Brandy shared the same fate we children believed had befallen us—living in the wrong family. Brandy's heart wasn't in destruction, it was in love. Endless, slobbering, knock-you-to-the-ground love. He was so starved for affection that if you gave him an absentminded pat, he would follow you around, his head nudging your hand, begging to be stroked until your fingerprints wore off. If you decided to deliberately give him some attention, say, a few minutes of neck rubbing and ear tickling, it would only inflame his desire. Patting Brandy was like deciding to dig your fingernails into a mosquito bite until it bled, only to discover the more you scratched, the more it itched.

Brandy was not our first pet. When I was five my parents brought home a case of Schweppes tonic water which, when they opened it, turned out to contain a black cat my mother named Schweppsy. Schweppsy and I immediately adored each other, so much so that when she had her first litter, she jumped on my bed in the middle of the night to deliver it.

Though we were not Catholic, my parents thought birth control was unnatural for any species, so our house was always filled with dirty diapers and newborn kittens. My brother and I got to name the growing brood of kittens. He wanted things like Ratfink and Killer, while I lobbied for Princess and Silky. We compromised with a literal approach, so Schweppsy begat Blackie, Whitey, and Grayie. I used to love holding them, massaging them like little balls of kitty dough in my hand.

Besides the cats, we continued to have a succession of minor, tragic pets. Our treatment of all these creatures should have gotten our house picketed by the Society for the Prevention of Cruelty to Animals. We had goldfish that generally didn't last quite as long as an application of lipstick. Mice, hamsters, parakeets all quickly expired due to our constant handling and inconstant feeding. What really got our attention was what happened to our pets after they died. We conducted elaborate funerals, then daily disinterred them, a band of elementary-school coroners studying gerbil decomposition.

By the time we got Brandy, Schweppsy had died, and we officially had three of her offspring, but more cousins appeared to be making a home in our unfinished basement. My parents had no plan on how we would introduce Brandy to the cats. They went with their inchoate belief in not interfering with what was natural. This philosophy appeared to be the result of a cursory reading of Dr. Spock, excessive viewing of PBS nature documentaries, and a longing to follow their own impulses. This longing had resulted in a teenage marriage and immediate reproduction. Now they longed to be free of the car pool circuit and the station wagon with fake wood siding that represented responsibility and repression. At least their animals could be free to rut and run.

It turned out that what is natural for cats to do when confronted with an unleashed German shepherd puppy is leave. The cats had always been allowed to wander in and out at will. We had no litter box or even set hours to feed them. Within a few weeks of Brandy's arrival Blackie, Whitey, and Grayie were no longer meowing at their bowl. Occasionally one of the cats would appear, like a phantom, and Brandy would run after it and it would take off across the yard. Then they stopped coming at all. I missed them and asked my mother where they were.

"They must have found a family that didn't have a dog," she said.

"Can we visit them? Can we get them back?" I asked. She said the cats had made their decision, and it was better to respect it than bother them in their new home. The ease with which the cats moved on made me both fearful and curious. Was it that easy to find a new family? And how did you know it was the right one?

Brandy was now our only pet, which didn't mean he got special care. He ran wild all day, menacing other cats and dogs, then spent the night docilely seeking our affection. He loved the yard next door—the couple would take turns ringing our doorbell, taking great umbrage that Brandy treated their carefully tended lawn as his bathroom. When they came to the door my parents responded to them the same way they responded to teachers who complained that we children weren't living up to our potential: "Why are you telling us? Go take care of it yourselves."

After a confrontation with these neighbors in which phrases like "Call the police" and "Throw the crap against your house" were used, my parents made an effort to keep Brandy inside most of the day. This both built up his anxiety and gave him the opportunity to go from room to room, looking for attention.

One of these afternoons my mother piled all of us in the car to go grocery shopping. Brandy barked piteously to be allowed to come, but we kept him in the house. It was a warm day and the French doors to the small second-story sun porch above the front door were open. As my mother backed out of the driveway, we saw Brandy run onto the porch and look at our receding car.

He put his front paws on the railing and howled. We waved to him. It was too much. As we watched, he backed up and took a running leap off the porch to the car.

He landed in the grass, crying and unable to get up. We jumped out of the car and went over to him; one of his legs was sticking out at a disturbing angle. Blood trickled from his mouth. We wrapped him in a blanket and gingerly put him in the back of the car as he whined and struggled. We were too shocked to speak. My mother drove him to the vet where they whisked him off still wrapped in the blanket. A little while later the vet came out. Brandy's leg was broken and he was badly bruised but miraculously there were no serious internal injuries and he would live.

He came limping home with a cast on his leg. For the first time we put him on a leash and took him on regular walks. We bathed him in affection. But something fundamental had changed in Brandy's relationship to us. I was disturbed by his level of suicidal devotion. Was this just the way dogs were, or had Brandy absorbed some of the melodramatic strain of my parents' marriage? It was not unusual for my mother to yell a parting shot at my father from that very sun porch. Did Brandy think it was a proscenium to be used for emotional displays?

Brandy was also changed by his experience. Although he enjoyed the new attention, it was as if he recognized there was something shameful, or certainly dangerous, about his needs. He began to want less from us. Eventually his cast came off and we let him back outside, collarless, to wander. One night, we noticed, after several hours of calling and whistling and searching the bushes with a flashlight, he appeared to have wandered off. My father put us all in the station wagon and we roamed the neighborhood calling out his name. He didn't appear the next day or the next. Even though we had never given Brandy what he needed, we were now distraught at his absence.

My father called the pound to see if he'd been brought in, no Brandy. The fourth day of Brandy's disappearance my father said he was going to put an ad in the paper and offer a reward. We children collected a pile of broken toys and stale Halloween candy to encourage the dognapper to release him. When my father opened the paper to see how to word the ad, he glanced at the "Found" column. He read aloud the description of a lost German shepherd with the same markings as Brandy. "That's him, that's him!" We jumped up and down and someone got the phone and my father made the call. When he hung up he said the people lived half a mile away and we would all go over and see. In the car my father warned us that we shouldn't get our hopes up, this dog might not be Brandy. "Can we keep the new dog, anyway?" my little sister asked.

We pulled up to the house, rang the bell, and the father came to the door. He was holding Brandy by the collar (they had gotten him a collar!). As soon as Brandy saw us he tried to lunge into our waiting arms. My siblings and I draped ourselves over him, so grateful to have found the dog we would soon be ignoring again.

My father took out his wallet.

"No, I'm just glad the dog found his rightful home," the other father said. He looked and talked like a TV dad—not the goofy kind, the kind you could rely upon to straighten out a mess. "He followed my son home from school. He had no identification, but we knew he wasn't a stray because he was well fed and well behaved. You've got a nice dog, there. Probably should have a collar on him."

"Good idea," my father said coolly.

As the two fathers stood in the doorway and we hugged Brandy, a pale, blond boy about ten came and stood near his father. He had obviously been crying. The father put his arm around the boy. The boy said, "Are they going to take King?" At the sound of the boy's voice Brandy turned. He started toward the boy, then looked at us—torn between the familiar mediocrity we offered him, and an uncertain but possibly dazzling future. The boy got on his knees. "Here, King." Brandy went to him and the boy buried his face in Brandy's neck.

The father tried to pull the boy off, but he resisted. Then the father spoke a little sternly. "King belongs to these people. You've got to let him go."

"But you said people who cared about their dog shouldn't let him run loose."

Brandy continued to let the boy pat him. The four of us looked at my father. We were going to lose this struggle just because we weren't good owners? By that criterion, we might not be allowed to return home and have to stay with this new family and their dog, King.

"Well, we better get Brandy home," my father said. "Thanks again for rescuing him." My father started to undo the collar.

"Keep it," the other father said.

Pulling him by the collar, we got Brandy to the car. He happily clambered into the back of the station wagon, discarding his identity as King as easily as I dropped my princess dress-up clothes on the floor. As we drove off the boy and his father stood in the doorway until we were out of sight.

Brandy slowed down and lost his wanderlust. Eventually, we children started going off to college, leaving just my youngest brother at home. By this time my parents' marriage finally had been put down. It was time for Brandy to be, too. My father, who hadn't lived at the house for years, came by to get my brother and Brandy for Brandy's final trip to the vet. They stayed in the room with him while the vet administered the injection. My brother said it was the first time he'd ever seen my father cry.

3

GENETIC IMPERATIVE

Sometimes the dog lover gene
skips a generation.

Once the house was emptied of children, it began to seem very empty, and vulnerable. My mother came home one day to find her bedroom ransacked and her jewelry gone. After this break-in she went for the electronic solution and had infrared burglar sensors installed all over the house that she tripped off every time she came down for a midnight snack.

She turned off the alarm and decided to get another dog, one fiercer than a German shepherd. She settled on an Akita, the Japanese dog bred to hunt bear. She named him Yojimbo, after the Kurosawa movie about a samurai sword slinger.

For the first time in her life my mother had her own dog. Yojimbo turned out to be everything my father was not: devoted, faithful, obsessed with her. Yojimbo and my mother were one of those couples who didn't need anybody else. Indeed, Yojimbo wouldn't allow anybody else—visitors to the house were in danger of being maimed. Yojimbo bit one guest on the forearm within minutes of his arrival. This man became my mother's last nonfamily visitor as Yojimbo's behavior sent her into a long reclusive period.

One of the most terrifying sights I've ever seen was the first time I met Yojimbo. I got out of the cab from the airport and as I walked up my mother's front steps the cat door flew open and a gigantic, gargoyle like head pushed through. The head was jerked back, and the front door opened. My beautiful mother was holding the straining animal at the collar. "I've told him all about you, he's so excited," my mother said as Yojimbo tried to drag her down to where I dropped my bag. I saw that Yojimbo was capable of enacting all the fratricidal fantasies children have when presented with a new sibling. "I'm going to let go so he can smell you," she said. I suddenly saw myself as a steaming corned beef. "Don't!" I said. But it was too late. He ran and sniffed me all over. I was prepared to see blood, but he settled for sticking his nose in my crotch.

That night I babysat for my six-month-old nephew. My brother and sister-in-law dropped the baby off at my mother's house, and while I was holding him, Yojimbo ran up and put his paws on my chest, jaws open, trying to locate my nephew's head.

"Mom, call him off," I screamed.

"He's a little jealous," she said. "Just let him smell the baby."

I could see I WAS JUST LETTING THE DOG SMELL THE BABY as the headline for the hideous newspaper story about what happened after I let Yojimbo get a whiff.

I said to my mother, "You've got to put Yojimbo in his pen."

"This is Yojimbo's house," my mother said. "I'm not making him spend the night outside."

I took my nephew to my old bedroom, Yojimbo following me up the stairs. Fortunately, as a teenager I had installed a hook and eye on the door as a privacy measure. I shut the door in the dog's face and dropped the hook in the eye. For the rest of the night, like a babysitter in a slasher movie, I cuddled my nephew while a tiny piece of metal stood between us and the wailing, straining Yojimbo. Every so often my mother called, "You're hurting Yojimbo's feelings!"

When we were growing up my mother had an active social life and was an avid moviegoer. But with the arrival of Yojimbo she gave all that up. She got into her bathrobe by nine P.M. to laze on the couch in front of the television, her companion dozing, but ever ready to attack, by her side. When we visited for holidays, we could barely coax her to go to a movie with us.

"By the time we park and they show all the previews, it will be three hours before I get back," she'd say. "I'd better not."

"If we walk him before we go, he should be able to hold it for three hours," I said.

"It's not that. He has a dog door to his pen. But if I'm gone too long, when I get home he's so upset and anxious that he just chews on his squeaker toy all night." Where did this come from? When we were teenagers she often didn't notice if we made it home at night.

Strangely, I was one of only four or five people Yojimbo met whom he didn't want to tear limb from limb. As with many male-female relationships my allure was based on my unavailability. The more my mother tried to baby-talk us into a relationship ("Oh, Jimbo, you love your sister, don't you. You are just trying to show your sister you missed her. Maybe your mean sister will rub you behind your ears the way you like and then she won't be such a mean sister anymore"), the colder I became. I suppose I could have discussed this dynamic with my therapist, but with all the outstanding issues to deal with, I didn't see how I could afford any sessions on interspecies rivalry.

I would give Yojimbo the most cursory of ear scratches then ignore him. This drove him mad. If during a visit my mother and

I were sitting in the den and she was giving him a full body massage, he would leave her embrace to come over and rest his muzzle on my lap, pressing it ever further into my legs until I gave him a pat of acknowledgment.

Once I flew in and stayed at my mother's because I was interviewing someone in Boston the following day. In the morning I sat on the bed, going over my notes, when Yojimbo walked in. I gave him my usual perfunctory greeting, but this time he wasn't going to take it. He walked to my other side and nudged me. Again I gave him a slight pat and said, "Jimbo, I have to work now—go away." He put his front paw on my lap and looked at me hard. I pushed him off, stood up and pointed to the door. "Out, Jimbo." He got the message and headed toward the door. I also got his message because on his way there he lifted his leg and urinated on mine.

When she heard my scream my mother came to the door. After finding out what had happened she tried to reprimand him, but was thwarted by her tears of laughter.

When Yojimbo died my mother was disconsolate. She wore a locket around her neck from which sprouted a corona of his coarse hair. It looked like a piece of jewelry you'd buy at Hogwarts. She had my brother bury Yojimbo in the front yard. Through her sobs she made my brother promise that when it was her turn to go, she and Yojimbo would be buried together. This presented a dilemma for my brother. He knew putting the dog in the front yard was a violation of the local health codes. He didn't want to contemplate having to put our mother there, too. But if she agreed to a more conventional final resting place, he doubted he could find a cemetery that would allow him to throw in the exhumed body of Yojimbo.

Yojimbo's death was liberating for my mother. She visited my sister in California. She stayed out for more than two hours at a time. But about a year after Yojimbo died my brother heard about a full-grown trained boxer whose owner could no longer care for him. My brother brought the dog to my mother for a visit, and instantly the leaden grief that she had never quite shaken dissipated. She named the dog Ali, and she was soon back on the couch in her bathrobe, with Ali slumbering next to her.

Fortunately for us, Ali was of a less maniacally possessive temperament than Yojimbo, so it was possible to bring grandchildren over to visit without worrying that Ali would see them either as threats or Meals Ready to Eat. When my four-year-old daughter came to visit, she immediately fell in love with him. That evening, while we were watching television, my daughter rested her head on Ali's stomach and they both went to sleep.

One night during the visit, after my daughter was in bed, my mother and I were watching TV when my mother pointed to Ali on the floor and said, "Look, look!" He was rolling over on his back and letting out an enormous yawn. She turned to me and said in a confidential tone, "Do you see now what I mean about him actually being part human?" It was true that as he let out a sigh and a snort and fell back to sleep, he did resemble my husband watching TV, but I felt a worm of fear when I realized my mother was quite serious. "He's a very nice dog," I said. She let out a little laugh, an acknowledgment that here was yet another example of a lifetime of mother-daughter failure to communicate. My daughter would have understood her. At the airport on our way home she began crying. "I miss Ali. I miss Ali. I want to be with Ali!"

A while later a crisis occurred in my mother's life when a vet diagnosed Ali with an enlarged prostate and strongly advised castration. I realized that if a doctor, after examining my father, had recommended the same surgery for him, my mother would have nominated the doctor for the Nobel Prize in medicine. But to suggest it for Ali was torment. She was afraid, she said, it would change their relationship. I cut off the discussion feeling we were going places better left unexplored.

My mother sent my daughter a photograph of Ali which my daughter put in a prominent place in her room. She often looked at it and reminisced. "I love it when I put my head on Ali and he makes a big sigh. It makes my head go up and down. When can we see Ali again?" Through me my daughter had inherited my father's dark deep-set eyes and my mother's dog-lover gene. And this genetic imperative would not be denied.

4

BED AND DOGFEST

My strange night in Wisconsin.

For most of my adult life, I'd had little contact with dogs. Few of my friends had them, none of my boyfriends, and I tried my best to avoid my mother's. It was on a reporting trip to a small town in Wisconsin that I had my most intense encounter with a dog before getting Sasha.

I could have stayed at the chain motel, bland though reliable, on the highway into town. Instead I found a bed and breakfast near the college where I was doing interviews. When I called, the owner said she had a room available, and added, "Oh, by the way, we have a dog, a sweet German shepherd. I promise you he won't be in your way, but I have to make sure guests don't mind dogs." The conversation reminded me of how long it had been since I'd even thought of Brandy. I said a dog would be fine.

When I arrived at the B and B, my hosts, a middle-aged couple, showed me around and gave me a key. They introduced me to their seventeen-year-old son, Brad, and to Packer, the German shepherd. Brad would be in charge of the house for the night.

He was an excellent cook and would make breakfast in the morning, they said. The host and hostess were going out of town to visit a sick relative. I should feel free to come and go. And I needn't worry about waking anyone else up. I was the only guest.

I went to dinner and when I got back to the house at eleven it was completely dark. Brad must be one of those industrious 4-H early-to-bed kind of teenagers, I thought. I tried to slip in without waking him, but the sound of the key in the doorway alerted Packer. He was thrilled to see me, jumping all over me and barking. I patted him and went to my room and he followed, still frantic for attention. I quickly got ready for bed and dragged Packer into the hall by his collar, shut the door and turned out the light.

I must have drifted off because a few minutes later I was awakened by the sound of Packer scratching and barking at the door. This was ridiculous—where was Brad? I had neglected to pack a bathrobe, so I put a raincoat over my nightgown and went down the hallway looking for Brad's room. It was easy to identify: football pennants, rock star posters, textbooks piled on a desk, a single bed. The bed was neatly made.

When we got to Brad's room Packer went in, circled, and whined loudly; he missed Brad. Well, Brad was a teenager, he'd probably be coming in late. "Settle down, Packer," I said. "Brad will be back." At the mention of Brad's name Packer barked louder.

I went back to my room, took off the raincoat, and got into bed. Packer was running up and down the hall, whining and barking. Sometimes the sound diminished as the dog made a circuit of the house. As soon as I started to doze, Packer was back at my door. Maybe he would settle down if I let him sleep with me. I opened the door and he bounded into the room. I patted the bed and called his name. He just snapped at the air. Finally, I took him by the collar and pulled him into bed with me. He bolted and fled down the stairs. It was not the first time I was unable to persuade a male to stay for the night.

By two A.M. Packer's barking changed to howling. It was obvious Brad was not coming home and Packer needed to relieve himself. I got out of bed, put on my raincoat, and went downstairs. Packer's leash was on a table in the front hall. He was jumping so much I had trouble getting it on him, but we finally went outside. It was a late-fall evening in Wisconsin and bitterly cold. I pulled my raincoat tight and Packer marched up and down the street. I was startled by how many pickups driven by men with bottles to their lips were out in the middle of the night. I wrapped my raincoat tighter.

My memory from walking Brandy was that dogs peed about every two and a half seconds, but Packer had a particularly resolute bladder. Up and down we marched, caught in passing truck headlights, for fifteen minutes. Not a drop of urine came out of Packer. I thought of letting go of the leash and saying in the morning I had no idea where Packer had gone—if anybody showed up to bid me bon voyage. Instead I hung on.

We went back inside. To the right of the main hallway was the living room, closed off by French doors. It had a sherry set on one table, fresh flowers on another, current magazines stacked by an armchair. I assumed the hosts served predinner drinks in there, when they were in town. I opened the glass door and Packer followed. He jumped on and off the couch and knocked the magazines off the table. I left him there and shut the door.

I went back to my room, took off my raincoat, and crawled back into bed. Because Packer was behind the living room door the howling was more muted. It was interrupted by the occasional crash, or sound of heavy furniture being moved. I dozed fitfully, waking every few minutes to what sounded like breaking and entering. Soon it was time to get up. I showered, dressed,

and went downstairs with my bag. I opened the living room door
and Packer raced out. A lamp was tipped onto the floor on top
of the magazines. An afghan, probably made by grandma, had
returned to its original state as a skein of yarn. A couch pillow
was leaking foam. There was a bad smell. Surely, I should feel
guilty, I thought, when I realized I didn't.

I closed the door and went into the kitchen. I found the dog
food in a cabinet and shook some into Packer's bowl. He inhaled
it, collapsed on the kitchen floor, and fell asleep. I started the
coffeemaker and made myself some toast. As I ate I was startled
by a noise behind me. It was Brad coming in the kitchen door.
Packer got up to greet him briefly then settled back to sleep. "He
must be tired," Brad remarked. Brad was carrying a bag of dough-
nuts. I said I'd just stick with toast. I finished breakfast and wrote
out a check. Brad took it, said thanks, then remembered something.

"Hey, was everything all right?"

"Just fine," I said. I patted Packer's head; he barely stirred. I
let myself out the back.

5

A BLANK SLATE

It's clear Sasha knows nothing about being a pet dog, and we know nothing about having one.

Monday morning, two days after we got Sasha, I was taking her on the first of her fifteen daily walks down the block, when up the block came a sight that so stunned me I felt as if I'd entered my own physics experiment. Some scientists believe our universe is just one of an infinite number, and that all the universes are floating around in membranelike bubbles. In other bubbles are versions of ourselves leading weirdly parallel lives. I must have jumped through one membrane and into another because coming up the street toward me was my neighbor Marius, who I knew did not have a dog, walking a beagle. (As long as I'm in a parallel universe, I thought, why does it have to be the one filled with beagles, and not the one filled with Swiss bank accounts?)

He must have had the same thought, because he gave me a slack-jawed, how-did-I-get-in-the-all-beagle-universe look.

We sputtered for a moment and finally he said, "When did you get a beagle?"

"Saturday. When did you get a beagle?"

"Yesterday," he said.

"I didn't even know you were looking for a beagle," I said.

"We weren't," he replied. "We were away at a resort and I saw her wandering around the property. As we were leaving she stood in the road blocking our way. I opened the door of the van and she hopped in."

By this time his wife, Leslie, had come down the stairs, looked at me with Sasha and screeched, "What's going on here?"

I explained that we had been beagle shopping for weeks and had just gotten our dog.

"If you want beagles, take ours!" she said.

Now my husband and daughter, going off to school, came down the street.

"What!" they exclaimed in unison, when they saw the two beagles, now doing a minuet of sniffing.

Leslie, speaking in ever louder, more agitated tones, explained that the whole family—they had three young children—had spent the weekend at an expensive resort in Virginia. They were putting their house on the market in a few days and Leslie, after spending weeks scrubbing and cleaning, wanted to keep her children from doing any damage.

"Now I have a stray beagle in my house!" she screamed.

She said that when Marius stopped the van she couldn't believe it. Within thirty seconds their oldest child, Ellen, had named the dog Loa. "Now she had a name!" Leslie continued. "I said, Marius, either this dog gets out of this van or I do. By then the kids were crying, saying, 'Mommy, we love Loa, can't we keep Loa.' And Marius was saying we can't just push this dog out to get hit by a car. So I got out of the van and just stood there."

"Then what happened?" I asked.

"Well, here I am, with *Loa*, and I have a house I'm trying to keep from looking like an animal shelter." At that point her youngest child came to the door calling out, "Where Loa, where Loa?" and Leslie went up to attend to her.

Marius bent down and gave Loa a pat. "She's been wonderful," he said. "She must have been someone's pet, she's already housebroken. She's a great dog." He went off to finish Loa's walk.

I couldn't believe this. I had invested endless hours in a dog search only to end up with an unhousebroken beagle, and my neighbors picked up a stray one who was already trained.

In a compromise, Leslie agreed to keep the dog if Marius agreed to board Loa at the vet's until the house sold. After they sold the house, it was weeks before they moved, and there was a wonderful period when we swapped backyards for beagle playdates. The two of them would chase each other incessantly, so that when the playdate was over, we would find the dogs spent and splayed on the patio.

One day I noticed Loa didn't seem to want to play with Sasha, and was backing away from her. When Marius picked her up he said that one of Loa's legs was bothering her and that he was taking her to the vet.

A few days later I ran into Leslie and asked how Loa was. "She has a bullet in her leg," she said, then added, "I didn't put it there!"

Loa was the real thing—a Virginia hunting dog who'd come a cropper of the hunter. Her surgery went well, but by the time she came out of the hospital, the family was ready to move. We were all sad to see them go, but Sasha was despondent. Every time I took her for a walk past their backyard fence, she'd go into a frenzy of sniffing and barking, longing for her missing friend.

BREW advised that before new owners got their beagle formal training, we simply let the dog settle into the household for about a month. Our settling in had certain features that reminded me of a new house settling into a foundation that turns out to have been built on a sinkhole.

For example, home security—which I had always thought of as protection from intruders—takes on a different dimension when you have a new dog. Either the dog is in lockup, or everything is battened down like a nuclear sub. Too late, I discovered my daughter's massive collection of stuffed animals should never have been left lined up, pert and cheery, in child-sized bookcases. Now we stumbled over their maimed bodies, plastic eyes ripped out and swallowed, giving them the look of victims in some Grand Guignol drama for the nursery-school set.

It's a mistake to think that just because Sasha has always ignored something it won't suddenly catch her interest. One day she figured out how to open the Velcro closure on my purse, the entire contents of which—lipstick, money, credit cards—were strewn over the front hall. Each item seemed to have been examined and rejected; I wondered if she had been seized by a sudden need for breath mints.

As with supervising small children, when your untrained dog is out of your line of sight you realize two things: sounds are bad, silence is worse. One day I was at my desk racing to finish an article on deadline. I gradually became aware of hearing from distant rooms rustling, tearing, the clip-clip-clip of Sasha going up and down the stairs, cats hissing, more rustling, then nothing. I stayed at my desk and finished my work. The silence had gone on for ominously long by the time I got up to investigate. As I turned to the stairs I saw that on each of the first five treads was a fresh poop, clearly the work of Sasha. I gingerly negotiated the rest of the way down. There was, I discovered, an absence of animals on the first floor.

They left evidence of their existence. The heavy kitchen drawer where I stored the cat food had been pulled open enough to provide access to the bag. There had been about three pounds of food in it, but a gash across the middle of the bag revealed only a few remaining pellets. In a Henry VIII–style banquet, Sasha had consumed one fifth of her weight in cat food. The food must have contained some special brain nutrients, since I then noticed that Sasha had managed to disable the brilliant string rubber band hook and eye contraption I had rigged up to keep the basement door open only wide enough for the cats to fit through. This had successfully kept the basement—and its litter boxes—cats-only territory.

As I descended to the basement I was struck by how quiet it was. I got to the bottom of the staircase to see the cats, utterly still, eyes fixed, staring down the corridor where we keep the litter boxes. Goldie and Biscuit looked as if they were watching a snuff movie. They were repelled, in shock, yet unable to turn away. At the end of the corridor Sasha had her front paws in a litter box, and was polishing off its contents, apparently as a palate cleanser. She heard me walk toward her and looked up. Our eyes met. I said nothing and did nothing. She ran past me up the two flights of stairs and into her crate. I arrived in time to see her retch the entire feast. I removed her, cleaned the crate, then put her back in. She promptly fell deeply asleep.

When I first became a beagle owner I learned that beagles are among the most commonly used dogs in animal experimentation because of their convenient size and agreeable nature. After this, I thought that Sasha could become a one-dog antivivisection league. I could just see her charging through the laboratory, smashing test tubes, eating the droppings of the other animal subjects, on her way to demolish the company cafeteria.

The crate was our first major dog accessory, bought at the recommendation of BREW. Neither my husband nor I had ever encountered one before—all our childhood dogs had roamed at will, humming "Born Free." The crate is a box with bars across it, used to contain the dog while it is being housebroken. Had I seen an animal in this in a pet store I would have called it a "cage." But the dog world decided "crate" had a more benign sound, as if your dog was a shipment of oranges nestled in raffia. You are told dogs perceive crates as cozy little dens, and Sasha did look snug taking a nap in hers. But upon awakening, she whined like a baby wanting to be rescued from a crib.

Once I let her out, there was the issue of the cats to deal with. I wasn't going to take my parents' route of allowing the dog to clear the house of cats in an act of feline cleansing. What I didn't expect was that the cats would get the upper paw. It turned out Goldie and Biscuit could be instructors for Delta Force. Without any apparent communication, each time they saw Sasha they walked toward her, then separated, maneuvering Sasha into a corner. Trapped, Sasha would start barking and nipping. The cats lunged, slashed at her ears, then scurried to a counter where Sasha couldn't reach them. To get even, when the cats were sleeping Sasha would sidle up to them and try to attack. Only she had nothing in her arsenal except her bark. The cats, aroused, would slash. To compensate, we lavished Sasha with attention, while the cats simmered in the background plotting revenge.

But nothing convinced me how much we were improvising as dog owners as the day after Sasha's first snowstorm. At best, Sasha was no fan of relieving herself in the rain, but she absolutely refused to go in the snow. My husband understood she needed to see dirt. He went out to our backyard and shoveled a foot-square patch. He had to explain to Sasha the reason for this snow-free zone, so carefully eyeing the windows of the neighbors on either side, he unzipped his pants and urinated on the newly cleared bathroom. He brought out Sasha who sniffed, circled, then squatted over the spot my husband had marked.

To understand Sasha better, I decided to see beagles doing what beagles were bred to do. According to Raymond Coppinger, co-author of *Dogs: A New Understanding of Canine Origin, Behavior, and Evolution*, about four thousand years ago people started following scent hounds—protobeagles!—on foot to find game, making this the earliest example of a working dog. The Patapsco Ridge Beagle Club, in southern Maryland, was hosting the modern-day equivalent, a field trial, so one rainy Saturday my family and I took off to see beagles in action. The club was in a large, low blue building decorated with paintings and engravings of that eternal pair: beagles and rabbits. A trophy board listed winners ("Tick Tock Blue") back to 1959. Out back, the beagles awaiting the chase, barking madly to get going, were held in small pens with open wire floors. We walked past the cages down the rolling expanse of soggy field. There stood a group of people in fluorescent slickers all facing a brush-filled valley. In the weeds we could see the white tips of two tails. We walked a little farther and two beagles, barely moving, their noses plastered to the ground, were howling as if they'd just found Rabbits of Mass Destruction.

The sixteen men and one woman—average age about sixty-eight—were holding long poles. I wanted to observe unobtrusively at first, so I tried to blend in with the other spectators. Since the other spectators consisted of my husband and daughter, the three of us, all holding umbrellas, began drawing a lot of suspicious stares.

My husband sidled up to me. "Dearest, are you nuts? Do you know you've got a Humane Society umbrella? These people are going to think you're here to shut them down." I switched umbrellas with him, but I had already made an impression.

One gentleman came over to me. "You're not some kind of tree hugger, are you?" he asked. "We don't mistreat them. They're working dogs." He indicated a large fenced area that held a few rabbits. "We spend four thousand dollars a year to feed these rabbits." He explained that not only do they not want the dogs to catch the rabbits, they don't even want the dogs to see them. "They get excited and they forget to put their noses down."

I introduced myself and explained that I was a beagle owner there to see beagles in action. His name was Joe O'Boyle, and he was an eighty-one-year-old plumbing contractor from suburban Maryland. I told him that when I thought of beagles hunting, I had an image of a pack of hounds, ears flying back in the wind, baying and running. Mr. O'Boyle explained that this field trial was about style, not speed. The dogs were not supposed to chase the rabbit, but inch by inch indicate where the little rabbit feet had touched. "We're looking for the dog running the line straightest, that's called 'painting the line,'" he explained.

The sport was a little like watching someone paint lines. It was both dull and strangely hypnotic, like Kabuki is to a Westerner. Mr. O'Boyle explained that the poles were for finding rabbits hiding in the brush. He was only running one dog today, an elderly one. "I have to get a new rotator cuff in April," he said, indicating his shoulder. "Then I'll get some young ones. Right now the young ones pull too much." He interrupted himself with a shout of "Tallyho!" I couldn't believe it. I thought "tallyho!" was something British people with titles like baronet, and viscount yelled on random occasions, a form of aristocratic Tourette's. I asked him what "tallyho" meant, and he told me it means you spotted a rabbit.

Mr. O'Boyle said beagle field trials were a great but dying sport—to prove it he swept his hand toward his vigorous but old compatriots. I asked why. "Where can you hunt rabbits anymore?" he said. "Most schoolteachers tell you, 'Poor little bunnies!'"

I started talking to another beagleman, Ewing Carhart, a retired power company employee. I said that if I brought my dog and took her off the leash, she'd be over the hill and gone. He was puzzled by this. "I have mine in a fenced yard, but if they get out, they don't go anywhere," he said. Three of his friends watched us intently. One called out, "Carhart, you keep talking to her. She's going to put you in jail, but we'll come visit." Another one added, "We'll bring you something real tasty to eat!"

After watching a few more rounds of sniffing beagles, my family and I went inside the clubhouse. On the counter of the kitchen was a home-cooked feast for $6 a person. Who knew the Patapsco Ridge Beagle Club was the state's best lunch bargain? When we sat down my husband said he had been listening to the conversation of the men settled on chairs on the porch. They were discussing great beagle sniffs of the past. A woman in the clubhouse was organizing a huge pile of *Hounds & Hunting* magazines. It has been published for over a hundred years, and describes itself as "The Beagler's Bible." She heard us and said, "These guys remember runs that happened forty years ago. Who was in it, how it came out, every detail. Of course they can't remember what they did yesterday."

One of the beaglers got a plate and sat down next to me, so I asked him if he thought we were crazy to have a beagle as a pet.

"My wife and I, we don't keep dogs in the house," he answered diplomatically. "No, no, we just can't see it. But not everyone feels that way. My brother-in-law, he and his wife have a rat terrier. It sleeps on the end of their bed." From his tone and facial expression I could tell that had he finished his thought it would have sounded something like, "Of course, my brother-in-law is a communist. And a vegetarian."

When we got home I saw I had been mistreating Sasha. As the first Queen Elizabeth might have told me, "Why dost thou thinkest thy beagle beguiles? 'Tis because it is of superior nose begot." I had picked a kind of dog used for its nose for as long as people had been using dogs, then I got mad at her when she went around the house smelling stuff. It was as if Pavarotti's parents had said to him as a kid, "Hey, Luciano, enough with the singing, already!"

Usually, when I walked Sasha, I moved as briskly as possible, tugging on her leash when she dug her nose into the grass. Now, I let her "paint the line." I could see she'd never win a field trial for straight sniffing. She took more of a cubist approach to "painting." I let her walk slowly so that she could take in all the rich aromas of our neighborhood. She seemed grateful.

6

BASIC TRAINING

*Sasha goes to obedience school and
becomes the class clown.*

When Sasha first arrived she did live up to the promise of being
completely unhousebroken. Ostensibly, I work at home. For the
first six weeks of life with Sasha my work consisted of walking
her endlessly and getting on my hands and knees to apply carpet
cleaner after she blithely squatted on the floor right in front of
me. Having a job that requires you to show up somewhere on a
regular basis seems inimical to dog ownership, anyway. I had taken
to asking the people I met at our local dog park what they did
with their dog during the day. Ninety percent answered that they
or their spouse worked at home.

On the housebreaking front, slowly things started to improve.
We took to saying to ourselves that Sasha was almost housebroken,
much like alcoholics who put off the first drink until after breakfast say they are almost sober. With the initial settling-in period over,
it was time to get Sasha some real training.

Every profession has its villains. Cops who sell drugs, surgeons
who remove the wrong kidney, lawyers who sleep during murder

trials, journalists who make stuff up (every story here is true!).
But as I looked for a trainer I recognized I imbued this profession with supernatural abilities. After all, you read very few articles about dog trainers gone bad: TRAINER TURNS CHIHUAHUA
INTO KILLER or OBEDIENCE LESSONS DERANGE DANDIE DIN-
MONT are not frequent headlines. Since I had no natural understanding of the dog mind, I was in awe of anyone who did. I
scrolled through the local trainers' Web sites. One woman promised only positive reinforcement and had classes coming up at a
nearby community center. My only concern was that she had
bipartisan endorsements from United States senators who had
used her services, and I am skeptical of anything a politician has
to say. Despite this, we enrolled.

When we arrived for the first in the six-week series, I had a
cat-person-with-a-dog sinking spell when the instructor, Eileen,
explained that dog training was a lifelong process. All I could
think of was the process of training our cats: "Fellas, here's your
litter box." End of training.

Eileen's philosophy could be summed up as "Will sit for liver."
The method of instruction was to teach via treat. Eventually you
wean the dog off the treat, giving it only randomly. But the dog,
like some slot-machine addict, keeps sitting in hopes each time
its rump touches the ground it will hit the treat jackpot. During
the first class I made the disconcerting discovery that I'm a prude.
No one else seemed bothered by spending an hour with their
hand in their dog's mouth—I was the only one who pulled out
a piece of tissue to wipe my fingers. I realized that I had never
digitally explored anyone's mouth the way I was Sasha's. But by
the end of the hour I was enjoying the feel of her Silly Putty lips.

At the class was a young woman who had also gotten a beagle—
actually a beagle-dachshund mix named Sigmund—which we recognized from the BREW Web site. As the weeks went on and

little Sigmund flawlessly learned "sit," "stay," and "come" while Sasha spent the hour sniffing her classmates, we thought of standing close to this woman, engaging her in conversation, surreptitiously exchanging leashes, then running off with Siggie.

During the classes my husband and I realized, as with everything dog related, that we were doing something wrong. Without a treat in hand we were unable to get Sasha to do a simple sit, yet Eileen could bring her into the center of the room, do something that looked like a gang sign with her fingers, and get Sasha practically playing the harmonica.

Despite Sasha's obvious need for a special education class, Eileen was kind and patient, encouraging our daughter to take Sasha's leash and try to teach her something. I talked to Eileen after class and she told me about her houseful of animals. Eileen was a dog lover but not exclusively. Besides her own border collie and giant schnauzer, she also had fish, a cat, two parrots—one imitated all the commands she gave to her dogs—ferrets, a snake, and for a while, rats. This last one is not unheard of in Washington, D.C., but Eileen had rats by choice. "The dogs were really mine and my daughters wanted a pet of their own. I knew rats were clean and very social, so they each got a pet rat," she said. "My daughter had one snuggle under her neck and sleep there all night." I was proud I was able to contain my gag reflex.

Eileen loved tricks and for homework told each of us to work on one to present at the last session. Little Siggie obeyed his owner's command to roll over and over, like a pig in a blanket careening off a serving tray. Other people had their dogs beg, or shake hands, or run in a circle. Then it was Sasha's turn. Eileen wanted a trick? How about this: I call Sasha's name and she runs in the opposite direction. However, by this time, I was able to get Sasha to follow the treat in my hand into a down position, then get her to scuttle a few inches toward it. I had the horrible thought that this was also a trick I could get one of Eileen's rats to do. But I didn't see—nor did Sasha—how scuttling translated into consistently peeing outside, or not eating my undergarments.

Sasha, along with the other dogs who actually got trained, was given a diploma. Since Eileen was so plugged into Congress, I thought of lobbying some of her congressional clients to pass a No Dog Left Behind Act. Instead I asked if she, or her assistant, were available for private lessons. They both said no. They suggested we keep working on what we had learned in class and that Sasha would come around. Since the housebreaking issue was causing me to go around the bend, my only hope was that Sasha and I would bump into each other as we made a circuit.

Shortly after the classes ended, I talked to another trainer who made me realize trainers didn't necessarily have all the answers. This woman had Ibizan hounds, and she told me that her dogs ate the downspout and the cable connection (fortunately not active) to her house. She had to build a fence a couple of feet from the foundation of her house to keep the dogs from destroying it. She built a separate fence around the gas meter. Then, to disguise all the fences, she decided to plant shrubs, but has ended up erecting a fence around each to keep the dogs from eating them. She said they did all this "just to aggravate me." Then she added cheerfully, "Dogs are a constant source of amusement." Yes, in the same way the classic movie short proved that a dinner party catered by the Three Stooges is amusing.

The natural history of Sasha's housebreaking was like that of the plantar wart. Months went by without recurrence, so I thought I had it beat, then I would feel something unpleasant on the bottom of my foot. My husband, daughter, and I took to making nightly trips through our house, shoulder to shoulder and barefoot, looking like police cadets combing a crime scene for shell casings, only we were searching for the latest squishy spot on the carpet.

It occurred to us that when you looked at Sasha's sweet face and exchanged glances with those melting brown eyes, you got the distinct sense that her brain had the size and electrical activity of a walnut. This conclusion, I found, was supported by science. In Raymond Coppinger's *Dogs*, he explained that research showed the first sixteen weeks of life were a critical period of development for the puppy. "Essentially, at sixteen weeks, the dog's social personality is set for life," he wrote. A dog's experience during the first few months determines the nerve connections between the existing brain cells. "A puppy that is raised in an impoverished environment has a smaller brain," he wrote. "It has the same number of cells, but not as many get wired together."

When I imagined Sasha's puppyhood, I saw her in a squalid pen, ripped from her mother's nipple so mom could get back on the hunt. It wasn't Sasha's fault and it wasn't our fault she was the way she was. She was like a personal computer that could do word processing but lacked an Internet connection.

Coppinger also wrote that one of the key developments in the transition from wolf to dog was the shrinking of the dog brain. A wolf needs a big brain to organize a pack hunt; a dog doesn't need one to sniff out a discarded drumstick. So, one of the most brilliant survival strategies of the dog was to get dumber. Coppinger described keeping wolves and dogs in the same type of kennel. The wolves watched intently how the humans manipulated the latch. On the first day in the kennel, there were always wolves who deduced how to undo their latch and then went to free their companions. With the occasional exception, the dogs simply waited for a human to open the latch. Year after year of watching the latch being opened will lead the dog to conclude that humans sure are good at opening latches.

For humans this reduction in intelligence was a plus. It meant we could tell dogs what to do. However, I was beginning to think Sasha was taking her evolutionary duty to be dim-witted to unnecessary lengths.

In a pet-advice newspaper column on keeping a dog house-broken and happy, a distinguished veterinarian recommended every dog get walked five times a day and also have at least one daily play session with other dogs. That sounds great, doc, so while I'm walking Sasha and chaperoning her social life, you can take care of the grocery shopping, the bills, the child rearing, oh, and making a living. Anyway, Sasha's inability to be completely housebroken wasn't due to insufficient walks. She now knew it was bad to go in the house, but to paraphrase the song, if going on the carpet was wrong, she didn't want to be right.

7

PROZAC, ANYONE?

Further adventures in training.

One night, my husband and I had dinner with a friend who'd also just gotten a dog from the pound. Hers was a perfect, little Labrador mix named Hannah. Within weeks she was housebroken and able to hang around the unfenced yard without a leash.

We started telling her about our troubles with Sasha.

"What kind of dog is she?" asked our friend.

"A beagle," my husband said.

At that she glanced furtively from side to side, leaned in, and spoke sotto voce, as if she was moved to confess that in her youth she had done prison time for running a methamphetamine lab. "We had a beagle when I was a girl," she said. "It never got housebroken. Apparently that's very common with beagles."

I began imagining how our house would look if I gave up on housebreaking Sasha, ripped out the carpet in the den, and replaced it with wall-to-wall sponge. No, I decided, I would not give in to genetic predetermination. Since I don't believe the day will ever come that we can order up a child who is a tall physicist with a great tennis serve, I know the day will never come that scientists will get around to fixing the beagle pee-in-the-living-room gene.

We were keeping Sasha, and we were going to get her house-broken. I turned to our veterinarian for help. Her recommendation was the same as always: run many expensive tests. When I argued that every expensive test I'd ever paid for had revealed that my animals were fine, she got the look that they teach the first day at veterinary school, before they even get to "the tailbone's connected to the hip bone." It's a look that says, "Sure you believe your pets are members of your family. Obviously you would let a member of your family die an agonizing death that a simple test could prevent."

Perhaps, the vet explained, the incontinence was caused by infection, infestation, diabetes, kidney stones, colitis, ureter or sphincter abnormalities. When the tests came back the vet pronounced with a grave happiness that everything was normal. "That's wonderful," I said, wondering if I would get a call from my credit card company about excessive activity, "but my house smells like it should be condemned."

"Yes, that. It now looks like it's a behavior problem," she said, furrows deepening. Well, you could run a lot of expensive tests to try to find out why I look the way I do in a bathing suit, but in the end it will come down to a behavior problem.

"I think it's time for psychopharmacology," she said, and pulled out a prescription pad. Since we had introduced them to Sasha, the cats had been exhibiting signs of stress-related colitis, so the vet suggested we put all three animals on meds. I hoped there would be medication left for the animals, once I filched enough to get me through this. "We'll start with Prozac," she announced. I was sure that in the Prozac entry in the *Physician's Desk Reference* there was nothing about it being indicated as a cure for the compulsion to relieve yourself on the dining room table (yes, Sasha did that), but then, what was?

Two weeks' worth of medication cost $200. Of course, if I'd gotten it prescribed for myself to treat my PIID (Pet Incontinence Induced Depression), insurance would have covered it. Still, I rationalized we'd be spending a lot more than that if our home was declared a Superfund site by the EPA. I knew the Prozac would take a few days to kick in, but I felt we were finally ready to turn a corner. A few days later we did, only we turned right into a case of explosive diarrhea from Sasha. It took me three hours to bathe Sasha, scrub down the house with bleach, and launder everything she had touched. I called the vet and she said, "Mmmm. You better stop the Prozac. You do see diarrhea in response to Prozac sometimes, but it is rare." Obviously it's rare or else half the population of the United States would be running around in Depends.

Sasha was such a shaking wreck that I wrapped her in a blanket and put her at the foot of our bed. I came and sat by her, patting her head during the day, and letting her sleep with us that night. She awakened my maternal instincts. She recovered quickly, and the episode seemed to make her feel more connected to us.

I continued medicating the cats. About a week into it I noticed that Goldie remained seated in his favorite chair in the den when Sasha came into the room. Instead of taking this lack of response as a blessing and going on her way, Sasha saw it as a challenge. Sasha came right over to Goldie, nudged him with her nose, and barked. Normally, this would have resulted in Goldie's riding Sasha bareback around the living room. But Goldie just waved his paw in a desultory manner. His message was clear: "Girl, you need to take an inward look at the source of your hostility."

I knew things were changing the day I walked in on a dog-and-cat mutual rectal appreciation session. I still harbored hopes I would see Goldie licking Sasha's ears while Biscuit kneaded her back, like the photo in one of my beagle books. I now knew this photo was either concocted through computer graphics, or done with dogs and cats recently returned from the taxidermist.

One day Sasha even came up to my office, whined, then ran and sat by the front door, showing she needed to go out. It was sort of like the scene in *The Miracle Worker* in which the young Helen Keller remembers the word for water. Sasha was worming her way into my heart, despite the cost of her worm prevention pills. My husband used to keep his toothbrush on the edge of the sink until Sasha stole five in a row, hiding them in her crate. There was something moving about looking in Sasha's crate while she napped and seeing her surrounded by her totems: my husband's toothbrushes, my daughter's stuffed sloth, the cups of my bra (the one whose straps she'd eaten).

In the evening we often found her curled up like an armadillo between our pillows. When we came in she pretended to be asleep, but we could see her open her eye a crack. My husband and I went through a big debate about whether to let her sleep with us.

It's not that I have a problem with animals on the bed. For twenty years I have slept with two successive sets of cats. But recently Goldie and Biscuit's sleeping privileges were in jeopardy since my husband had started complaining the cats were keeping him awake. I'm a light sleeper and they never woke me up, so I couldn't understand how they were bothering him.

"In the middle of the night they run up and down my body, then they sit on my chest and crush it," he said.

"It's hard to believe I wouldn't be aware of any of this," I said.

"Do I have to install a video camera? They march up and down my body all night like they're on a picket line, then they sit on my chest. They're driving me crazy."

Ever the considerate wife, I suggested he might be having nocturnal psychotic episodes.

A few nights later, cats still in the bed, I got up at four A.M.

to go to the bathroom. When I returned there was Biscuit, all nine-teen pounds of him, sitting in the middle of my sleeping husband's chest, peering into his open mouth as if about to perform peri-odontal surgery. Goldie, all sixteen pounds of him, was climbing up my husband's legs. I was shaken. It was painful, but I agreed the next morning to banish the cats at night to the basement.

So we had an opening. The problem was we were worried how Sasha would fill it. Let's just say there was a day with Sasha that was so bad I just wanted to get into bed and pull the covers over my head, but was dissuaded from doing it when I discovered she had peed on the mattress. On another bed-wetting occasion it was so late at night—we had just cleaned up from a dinner party—that we piled towels over the offending areas and tried to pre-tend we were in a water bed that had sprung a leak. But several months had gone by without any mattress marshland, and we thought letting Sasha spend the night might bring us closer.

I found out that some trainers think sleeping with your dog is a critical error with long-term consequences, like giving brandy to quiet a cranky baby and ending up with an alcoholic teenager. The belief was that bed-sleeping destroys the owner's standing as pack leader. Since I sleep much better when there's an animal in the bed (in addition to my husband), I interviewed some veter-inary behaviorists about this. They reassured me that sleeping with an agreeable dog was fine, and should not provoke any status anxiety in either dog or owner.

So we invited Sasha aboard. There is some tension between the desires of the two sleeping species. She's looking for that atavistic, bodies-piled-in-a-cave feeling. We're looking to not wake up to beagle snout. She will only settle at the end of the bed if she is positioned atop the blanket between my feet. Then, as the night progresses, she slithers upward, in a procedure that resembles reverse childbirth. Before dawn, I have to redeliver her to the foot of the bed. Otherwise, she has been a fine sleeping companion.

Despite all the progress, we were still plagued with setbacks. One night after we put our daughter to bed my husband came downstairs, flopped on the couch, and started reading a magazine. He fell into the state of twitching half-sleep that characterizes all airline passengers traveling without children. I puttered around the house and an hour later came into the den and sat down, which woke him up.

"It stinks in here," my husband announced.

"Please, I can't take it anymore."

"Really. There's something wrong in this room."

I got up with a heavy sigh and surveyed the rug.

"I don't see anything," I said. "I don't smell anything, either. I think it's your imagination."

"I'm telling you, it stinks," he said.

"Then you look for it."

My husband sat up. As he did a dog turd fell off the back of his shirt. He was less upset than relieved he wasn't losing his mind.

I thought of going back to our original trainer and suing her the way parents sued school systems for graduating their illiterate children. I despaired to a couple of friends about ever getting Sasha fully trained. They each told me that their dogs were transformed from bed-peeing, house-destroying scourges into, if not Rin Tin Tin, then decent pets. To do this, I had to see one man, their dog trainer, Todd.

8

SATAN VOMIT AND EAR FLUBBER

My sister had the world's worst dogs.

Whenever I felt blue about how far we had to go with Sasha, I thought, well, she's not Knut or Paris. These were the two dogs that consumed my sister's early adulthood. My sister's dog-loving gene definitely could have used gene therapy.

The first signs of pathology manifested themselves during her nursery school years. A lot of children go through a phase, which can last hours, or even days, in which they pretend to be an animal. My sister, Liz, at age four declared she was a dog, and wasn't ready to let go of this belief until my mother told her she had to walk upright, and not on her hands and knees, to kindergarten.

When Liz finished college she and her soon-to-be-husband, John, moved to Seattle and immediately decided to get a dog. "I loved dogs and we were young and irresponsible," she recalled. They got a giant book listing breeds and Liz marked the pages that said things such as "friendly and people-oriented," while John folded the pages with descriptions such as "fierce," "highly protective."

They compromised on a Belgian shepherd they got from a

breeder who said that when their dogs got out of control, her husband settled them by spraying them with a hose. Liz and John had been English majors, so they named the puppy Beowulf, after the mythical hero of medieval literature. Beowulf the puppy lacked the brio of Beowulf the prince. Because of his early hosing, he was phobic around men and cowered whenever John came to him. John was like the overbearing military father in *The Great Santini* and was infuriated that his little male dog was a wuss.

They wanted Beowulf to sleep outside in a shed, but each night he keened at the moon, so John went out and told him to shut up. Finally a kind but exasperated neighbor explained that the two of them were actually teaching the dog to be frightened and noisy and that they needed to get professional training. John decided he was finished with Beowulf. Amazingly, they had befriended a couple who also had a dog named Beowulf, and the couple offered to take Liz and John's Beowulf. Liz loved the dog, but felt he would be happier in a more stable home. To avoid confusion the adopters changed Liz's dog's name to Beo and their own to Wulf.

Dogless, Liz and John went to visit our mother. While there, our mother's Akita, Yojimbo, clearly wanted to kill John. They saw Yojimbo menace the mail carrier. My mother told them about how Yojimbo tried to attack any animals that came on the property. John decided an Akita had the temperament he wanted. When they returned to Seattle they started looking for one.

They found a breeder who had a litter of puppies ready to go. When they observed the dogs, one was dominating his littermates. "That's the one," said John. They named him Knut, after the Scandinavian king who briefly ruled both Denmark and England. The puppy was adorable, and each morning bounded to their bed. John became obsessed with Knut's size. He wanted Knut to reach twenty-eight inches, but it looked as if this dog might be a runt, which infuriated John. "The way he was obsessed with measuring Knut made me realize that I could never have a child with John," recalled Liz.

Once when Knut was still a puppy, they took him on one of their extreme vacations, this time hiking up a glacier. During their ascent, Knut lost his footing and slid into a gorge. Liz became hysterical but John was blasé. "He has to learn to be tough," he said. Liz watched in anguish as Knut laboriously made his way back to them.

As Knut grew, it became clear that he didn't have a guard dog's temperament. Sure, if not restrained he would kill any passing cat or small dog, but he loved people. Once Liz and John were coming back from a basketball game and were stuck in horrendous traffic. Behind them some kind of altercation had taken place between two drivers who had now abandoned their cars, one chasing the other with a lead pipe. The guy with the pipe smacked it into John and Liz's car during his pursuit, which caused Knut to look out the window with great interest at the passing show. He never even barked.

"That was it for John," said Liz. "This was dereliction of duty." John started searching for a real watchdog, something fiercer than a bear hunter, something more along the lines of a canine Hannibal Lecter. John considered a pit bull, but decided they were too docile. He settled on a fila Brasileiro, a breed distinguished for its highly exclusive listing in the Dangerous Dogs Act of Great Britain. European countries that allow filas in the show ring forbid the judges from getting in touching range of the dog.

Although they probably would have had better luck finding ads for filas in *Soldier of Fortune* than the local newspaper, amazingly one day a classified for fila puppies appeared. Liz and John immediately drove out to the country to see the dogs. The breeder was a disheveled old man with rheumy eyes and a liquid cough. He shambled out back to where he kept the puppies caged. As soon as the dogs caught sight of Liz and John they went berserk, barking and scratching at the bars. John was thrilled.

The owner reached in the cage and brought out the puppy he said would be perfect for them. "I didn't even think this breed was a good idea, but when the guy brought out the puppy I really got worried," said Liz. His navel was so distended it looked like he'd swallowed a thumb that was now working its way out. Like the breeder, the puppy had runny eyes, respiratory problems, and something wrong with his gait. "Filas are supposed to move like jaguars. This one shuffled around like a crocodile," Liz said. She expressed her concerns to the breeder.

The man explained that not only was he a breeder, he was a psychic. Through a psychic assessment, he was able to divine that this dog was destined to be a champion. Since the American Kennel Club refuses to recognize the breed, the meaning of "champion" was unclear. As to the dog's specific problems, the breeder explained the herniated navel would heal itself, the swollen eyes and respiratory problems were the result of a cold and would soon clear up, and the walking thing was just a stage the dog would outgrow.

What happened next proved the breeder did indeed have the gift of second sight. He saw that these two naïve nitwits were going to buy his ill-bred killer.

"How much is he?" asked John.

"Six hundred dollars," said the breeder.

"Will you take a check?" asked John.

On the drive home Liz found herself as moved by the pathos of the little creature as John was by his potential for mayhem. In keeping with their literary leanings, they named the dog Paris. The reference was to the character in Greek mythology who caused the Trojan War. It turned out the psychic breeder was right about one thing: the herniated navel cleared up on its own. However, Paris's eye troubles weren't due to a cold but a condition called "entropion," which causes the eyelids to curl inward resulting in agonizing irritation. It was incurable, but relieving the symptoms required daily application of gloopy medication. One eye permanently drooped, giving Paris a Quasimodo look. His walking difficulties were due to hip dysplasia. That was curable. The cure took six operations costing a total of $10,000.

Other problems emerged. One day the neighbors in the apartment below them came upstairs to complain about the sound of heavy machinery being run in their apartment at odd hours all day and night. Liz and John had no idea what they were talking about, until they realized it was Paris. He lay on the floor and snored at a supersonic decibel level because of chronic nasal blockage. "When he snored, he looked like a cartoon puppy with his lips flapping, 'poot-poot-poot,'" recalled Liz.

When Knut, their Akita, first met Paris, Knut was an adolescent and Paris was a puppy. Knut grappled with the puppy, put Paris underneath him and humped him. Welcome to Attica. Liz and John soon realized their apartment was not sufficient space for two soon-to-be-huge dogs. And John wanted to have a backyard for them to run and play in. They bought a small house, and kept the dogs outside most of the day.

By this time Paris was entering his adolescence and his personality was jelling. He had both an aggressive and a hypersensitive nature. Once Liz took Paris for a walk and a couple out with their seven-month-old infant saw Paris. The father took his child out of the stroller and held him over Paris, saying, "Look, a doggy. Say hi to the nice doggy." The nice doggy's afflicted eyelids popped open and he began salivating and growling. "I was able to get him away because he wasn't yet full grown," says

Liz. "If he had been, that kid would be dead." That ended Paris's walks—from now on he was only allowed in the backyard.

But Liz soon discovered that he was easily overstimulated. The sight of a butterfly, the feel of a passing breeze, would send him into hours of barking. The neighbors complained bitterly, but John refused to address the problem, adding to growing tension in the marriage. Liz considered having Paris's vocal cords cut, but she couldn't bring herself to do it. She got him an electric collar, which gave him a shock each time he barked. This led to hours of the sound of "Woof-woof, a-ooooo!" as the jolt kicked in. Liz realized she would have to set the collar at "electrocute" for it to have any effect.

By the time Paris was a year old, it was evident that his disturbing physical appearance was permanent. He was a huge dog, around 130 pounds, and his head was disproportionately massive, with enormous slobbering jaws. His body was thick and muscular and ended with a long, ratlike tail. "He looked like Peter Boyle in *Young Frankenstein*—a creature made of parts that didn't belong together," Liz said. His facial expression was a combination of torment, confusion, and desire to be loved.

When our grandmother visited Liz the first time after she got the dogs, Liz put them outside, fearful that an enthusiastic dog greeting would result in our grandmother requiring hip surgery. As Liz and our grandmother were sitting in the living room, our grandmother looked outside and caught a glimpse of Paris. After a sharp intake of breath she said, "No. No, that can't be!" The first time I met Paris I concluded he was the long-sought evolutionary missing link between reptile and mammal.

His malformed body and psychotic personality faded into the background of his most noticeable problem: his odor. A stench, really, coming from every part of him. This wall of stench permeated the house, the car, everywhere he went. Friends described it as "primordial hell soup" or "Satan vomit." One friend suggested Paris's anal glands must be blocked and that Liz should take Paris to the vet to get them expressed. It turned out they weren't blocked; they were simply expressing themselves. When I visited, I helpfully pointed out that her dog reeked. By this time she was so defensive she said, "That's just the way dogs smell."

"If that was the way dogs smell, then skunk would have become man's best friend," I replied.

Liz asked the vet for a diagnosis, but all he could come up with was, "Your dog sure is a stinker." Liz bathed Paris frequently, and paid rates equivalent to a makeover at the Canyon Ranch so a groomer would risk life and limb to do the job. The lack of smell would last at most a few hours. Liz tried deodorizing Paris herself, swabbing him with essential oils. All that resulted was a stench with a top note of lavender.

Liz and John could have few friends over. Those Paris didn't like he wanted to dismember. Those he liked had it worse. He bathed them in the foul foam he constantly produced from his muzzle.

A few days after Paris returned home from one of his leg surgeries, Liz noticed that his smell was even more outrageous than usual. She went over and started sniffing him. It was all dreadful, but one of his bandaged legs was unbearable. It turned out the leg had been wrapped too tightly and gangrene had set in. It had gone undetected for three days because of the background stink. He survived, but had a hole in his leg for the rest of his life; it never bothered him. After another surgery he was supposed to be confined and immobile so his hip could heal. But a cleaning woman at the vet's office accidentally left his crate open and he escaped from the animal hospital. The vet found him racing down the street on his damaged leg and captured Paris just as he was about to kill a small dog.

About this time Liz and John's marriage broke up. Although the dogs had been John's idea, he had no intention of caring for them while launching his bachelorhood, so he left 115-pound Liz to care for more than two hundred pounds of uncontrollable dogs.

Full grown, Knut weighed about eighty pounds. Once Paris surpassed him in size, the balance of power shifted in Paris's favor. Now Knut had to submit to Paris's desires. Knut's dethroning coincided with the development of a virulent skin condition. Knut lost much of his magnificent, thick coat and was covered with sores. The veterinarians were not able to find a cause or cure, but gave Liz repellent ointments to apply daily.

Paris loved Knut. Over the years it became apparent that Paris felt for Knut the love that dare not bark its name. Paris adored licking Knut. He started with Knut's ears. With the pleasure of attending to Knut, Paris's teeth chattered, his muzzle foamed, and his eyes bulged, or at least bulged as much as possible with ingrown lids. Knut stoically allowed the licking to progress until Paris got to Knut's genitals. At that point Knut wavered between pleasure and annoyance. Finally, Paris attempted to mount Knut, and Knut turned and bit Paris's neck. They wrestled viciously until Liz hit them with a broom to break them up. Then the cycle started again. She felt as though she was living in an endless episode of HBO's depraved prison drama, *Oz*.

Because she couldn't leave them outside all day, the basement became the dogs' territory. While down there they started getting into pissing matches. Real pissing matches. One dog would release about a gallon of urine and the other would see if he could top that. "The basement became a toxic waste site," said Liz. Despite everything, Liz adored her dogs; she knew no one else would.

I was living in northern California when Liz's marriage broke up. Shortly afterward, I went to Los Angeles for a job interview and suggested Liz fly down from Seattle to meet me there. She could forget about her marital and dog troubles and have a weekend of fun. Over breakfast the second morning of the trip she remarked that her left hand suddenly felt numb. She put it to her face and said that felt numb, too. Then she stood up, and her left leg gave way and she fell to the floor. "I think I'm having a stroke," she said. She was thirty years old. I called an ambulance and in the emergency room the doctor told me she had indeed had a stroke. A neurosurgeon later came out and said she had a malformation of the blood vessels in her head and they had burst. She had lost the use of her left arm and leg and needed brain surgery that night.

She was in the hospital for two months. To help her, I moved into the spare bedroom of a wonderful family friend. Miraculously, Liz retained all her mental functions, and over the weeks she slowly learned to walk again. She had left her two dogs behind and I had left my two cats. Through phone calls to neighbors and friends, we arranged makeshift care for our animals and tried not to think about them. "I know that my stroke was because of a congenital condition, but part of me wondered if caring for those dogs hadn't sent me over the edge," she said.

When she got home, John moved back in to help her, and they tried to patch up their marriage. Their home, which had been left to the dogs, smelled like a charnel house. When Liz arrived she discovered Paris had gone lame for the sixth time because of his hip problems. John suggested she just have him put down. "There I was limping around with a cane, and his response to lameness was a fatal injection," she said. "I knew we'd never make it." John moved out and they eventually divorced.

Liz slowly healed. She took to walking Knut, which was good therapy. Before her stroke she was a casting director in Seattle and she became friends with a young local actor she thought had promise. Since he was only working sporadically she hired him to help her fix up the house and to take care of the dogs. His name was Brendan Fraser, and not long afterward he moved to Los Angeles and became a movie star.

Unlike anyone else besides Liz, Brendan had affection for Paris. When he took the dogs out back he brought a couple of tennis balls to throw to them. Paris was in heaven, catching the ball and covering it with his stinking slobber. One day, when Brendan was hosing out the basement, he noticed that the water made Paris cower in fear. Brendan developed a diabolical game. He would hold the tennis ball in one hand and Paris jumped and bayed in excitement. Then with the other hand, he picked up the hose and Paris quaked. Brendan slowly brought his two hands together, until the hose was cascading water over the ball, thus completely fritzing out Paris's limited mental capacity. "Ball good. Water bad," Brendan said over and over, adopting a doofus voice that he later used to great effect when he played "George of the Jungle."

About a year after her stroke, Liz started dating. Because she couldn't remove Paris's odor from her home she decided to think of it in mythical terms. A man had to fight his way past her beasts—and their smell—in order to be worthy of her. The man who became her live-in boyfriend said he knew he was falling in love with her the day he stopped feeling sickened by Paris.

When Paris was five he developed an incurable wasting disease. As usual with Liz's dogs, the vet could not diagnose the source of the problem. Paris stopped eating and spent the night howling in pain. "I knew he was doomed from the time he was a puppy," say Liz. "In the morning he would come to my bed with the little blanket he slept with—you cannot imagine the rankness of this blanket—and the word 'doom' would ring in my head. But no one else would have loved Paris the way I did."

Although her devotion to this beast did not transform him into a prince, or even a dog anyone else could stand to be in the same room with, she was grief-stricken when he died.

That left Knut. Liz feared Knut would mourn the death of his companion, but he didn't seem to notice. He was too consumed with the agony caused by his chronic skin inflammation. He was covered with oozing sores that he couldn't stop gnawing. Liz developed a tic, calling out, "Knut, stop! Knut, stop!" whenever she heard anything that sounded like chewing. Every so often a new treatment worked, the sores cleared, and he was magnificent. Then like something out of Cinderella, the clock struck twelve, the medication stopped working, and Knut was turned into a scab-covered pumpkin.

Finally an effective oral medication came on the market. The side effect, however, was incessant intestinal gas. Just when her house was beginning to clear of Paris's odor, Liz was back where she started. Once I came to visit. We had had a long day and were looking forward at night to watching a movie and eating ice cream sundaes. We had just settled down on the couch, when Knut erupted with the sulfuric content of Vesuvius. We spent the rest of the evening watching the movie with dishtowels draped over our noses.

When he was eleven, Knut developed another condition that defied medical treatment. His ears started producing copious amounts of odiferous, greenish-brown, waxy slime. To get rid of it he would whip his head around, spreading goo on whoever or whatever was in its path. It reminded Liz of flubber. Again, she turned to her vet for help. "He's got an enormous amount of smelly wax, that's for sure," the vet said. He could provide neither reason nor cure. Liz cleaned out Knut's ears daily; she contemplated suicide. But she realized if she were gone, no one would care for her dog.

About a year later Liz went on a week-long vacation. By this time, besides his sores and his wax, Knut was deaf and arthritic. She boarded Knut at a veterinarian's office because she wanted him to be able to get proper medical care while she was away. When she returned, she dropped off her bags at home before going to pick up Knut. There was a message for her from the vet's office: "Please call us before you come." She called. The receptionist asked her to hold while she found a doctor. A vet she had never spoken to before got on the line.

"Hello, this is Dr. Williams," he said. "I'm very sorry to have to tell you that . . . that—Coot? Nut? Cut—"

"Knut!" said Liz.

"Yes, Knut. I'm sorry to have to tell you that Knut has died."

The day before his intestines had twisted; his end was swift. The vet told her that older dogs often die while their owners are away, as if they want to spare them the pain of witnessing it.

She was heartbroken, but as time went on, especially as she spent months scraping newly discovered deposits of ear wax off the walls, she felt she had been given back her freedom.

A year later, my husband was in Seattle on business and Liz picked him up at the airport. I had told him the stories about her late dogs: the foam, the stench, the sores, the wax. He thought I was exaggerating. Then he got in her car.

"My God! What's that smell?" he asked.

"My dogs," she said.

"I thought they were dead," he said.

"They are," she said.

"Well," he replied. "We'll always have Paris."

9

"YESSIR, TODD, SIR, YOUR MAJESTY"

Sasha meets her match.

I approached Todd's dog-training class with trepidation. I feared that yet again, Sasha would be the worst student. Todd's classes met at several outdoor locations around the city. They were ongoing, so all you had to do was show up with your dog and pay $15. I took Sasha one Sunday morning to the meeting place in front of a pool hall half a mile from our house. It was a scene out of every basic-training movie, a motley group of misfits trying to follow the drill sergeant. Todd was an imposing presence at about six feet three, 240 pounds, with a shaved head. He was African American and bore more than a passing resemblance to Shaquille O'Neal. He traveled with his rottweiler, Morgan, who followed him, worshipfully, off-leash.

After Sasha and I took our place in the line of about a dozen dogs and owners, I got in a conversation with the people on either side of me. It quickly became apparent most of them were Todd veterans. One said, "I've been coming to Todd for years." Maybe dog trainers were like Woody Allen's therapist; or maybe dogs were like Woody Allen—a cure is out of the question.

Todd told us to have our dogs sit, then we were to walk to the end of the leash, and turn our backs. The dogs were supposed to stay seated. All the dogs, from the Labrador mix, to the Great Pyrenees, to the other beagle (!), obeyed. Ready to give Sasha her commands, I got the same queasy feeling as when I turned to the math portion of the SAT. Sure enough, Sasha would do no more than bounce her rump on the ground, get up, and wander around. Todd came over.

"What's going on here?" he said.

"My dog can't do this," I said.

"Do you mind?" he said, taking the leash from me. He gave it a quick, downward snap. "Sit," he said firmly. She sat. He then put his hand in front of her face and told her to stay, and walked to the end of the leash. She stayed.

"Your dog just made a big mistake," he said. "She showed you she understands."

As soon as Todd walked away, Sasha was up, trying to wander. At the end of the class we all walked to an empty tennis court, where the dogs were taken off-leash and allowed to socialize for a few minutes. Sasha ran to the periphery of the court, tail so far between her legs it was touching her belly. Occasionally another dog came along and tried to sniff her, and Sasha ran. She looked like an Enron accountant during an outing at the exercise yard at Sing Sing.

At the end of class someone had a question that started with "My dog wants—" and Todd cut him off. "Oh, so your dog has opinions," said Todd. "See Morgan here." Morgan looked up at his master. "He had lots of opinions when I first got him. Now you know what his opinions are? What I tell him they are!" Since I have been unable to get my husband to share my opinion that the hamper is superior to the floor for storing laundry, I doubted I could achieve this level of mind-meld with Sasha.

Sasha and I continued to go to classes, and the same pattern prevailed. When Todd took her from me she obeyed, when he gave her back to me she didn't. Finally, during a down-stay, in which all the other dogs looked as if they were sunbathing at St. Tropez, and Sasha and I looked as if were entered in a Greco-Canine wrestling competition, Todd came over and said, "I think I should do a house call."

On the appointed day, Todd rang the bell, and Sasha ran to greet the new visitor. When I opened the door and she saw it was Todd, she sat, looked at him wide-eyed, and started shaking. Her thoughts were clear. "Not in my house. Not T-Todd." Todd told me to put on her leash. He took the leash and sat in the living room. Without a command, she sat, still shaking. He asked what had been going on with her.

I explained that she relieved herself all over the house, including twice on our bed. That she ran away when we said come, that she jumped up on the dining room table, that she tipped over the garbage can.

"Why are you letting her do this?" he asked.

"I'm not letting her, I—"

"You have an unhouse-trained dog that you've given roaming privileges."

"I know, but—"

"There are three places this dog should be. On the end of this leash"—he gave a little tug and Sasha started shaking in double time—"in her crate, or in the fenced yard. That's it."

"But she doesn't like being in her crate and—"

"She doesn't like being in her crate!" he said, raising his voice. "Where was this dog before you got her?"

"She was in a shelter in West Virginia. They were going to euthanize her."

"She was on death row in West Virginia and now she's living here." He swept his arm around our living room. "And she gives you those droopy beagle eyes and you feel sorry for her! She's won the doggy Powerball! Her life is better than yours! All you're asking is that she doesn't pee in your bed, but you think that's too harsh!"

He had a point.

He instructed my daughter to get a bath towel which he folded into thirds. He put Sasha on it. "This is her classroom. This is where she's going to learn to be a dog." He told us when she wasn't outside or in her crate, we should have her on the towel while one of us held the leash. This seemed to fall within canine Geneva Convention guidelines.

Todd stayed for an hour and talked about his twenty-five years as a dog trainer and his history. He was from Charlestown, West Virginia, but grew up in Washington. His whole family was from the area. They came from so far back that Todd said on one side he was descended from one of George Washington's slaves. As Todd talked, Sasha, thinking he wasn't paying attention, would attempt to wander off the towel, but he would immediately snap the leash and return her to sitting. Then he had me take the leash. As he stood to hand her off, Sasha gazed up at him and appeared to be in the process of being electrocuted, so wildly was her body twitching. At the end of his first session Todd announced, "I can already tell she is the fourth best beagle I have ever trained." I couldn't bring myself to ask if he had only trained four beagles.

The next day I set Sasha up on the towel next to my desk. At first she kept trying to wander, but eventually she became resigned and seemed to settle down. When I stood up to go get some coffee, about two feet of leash, unattached to dog, came along with me— Sasha had chewed through it. Round one to Sasha. I got a new leash, kept an eye on her, and it was soon clear containment worked—there was no opportunity for accidents in the house. In response to this severe new regimen, Sasha became the chief lobbyist for the Homeland Bladder Resistance Act. Instead of relieving herself as soon as we got outside, Sasha would now hold it while we circled and circled and circled the block. "You don't want me to go," she seemed to say. "Well, fine. I'm not going."

One Saturday, about a month after I started this new training routine, we were at group class. When it came time to tell our dogs to get down, then walk away and turn our backs, Sasha went down and, peeking over my shoulder, I saw that she stayed in place. What's next, Hugh Hefner declares he prefers the company of women his own age?

She stopped pulling on her leash, sat when I instructed her. We stopped finding wet spots in the house. She relieved herself quickly on walks. She was getting trained! I expected to hear any day that *Playboy* magazine had started an editorial crusade to ban breast implants.

10

A PLEADING E-MAIL

I answer it and my husband
finds happiness.

Thanks to Todd, some days life with two cats and a dog was serene. Then I got a pleading e-mail. It was not the usual pleading e-mail that explains access to your bank account will make the world a better place. This one was a mass mailing from Laura, the head of BREW. It said due to a particularly cold winter, hunters had been wildly abandoning beagles and the organization was swamped with rejected dogs. She was begging for BREW families to take in foster beagles.

I went to their Web site and saw dozens of needy beagle faces. I called my husband and he said, "Go ahead and get one if that's what you want." I wrote back to Laura saying we would take a foster beagle, begging that we get a dog who at least had a clue about housebreaking. I realized as soon as I hit "send" that my husband could print out this e-mail and make it Exhibit A if he ever tried to have me involuntarily committed.

Within minutes, Laura wrote back suggesting I drive to a veterinarian's office an hour away and get Roscoe. I looked him up on the Web site, and read his Boy's Town life story. He had been found wandering in the woods of rural Virginia by a man who then placed him in a temporary home. When that family decided they couldn't care for him anymore, he was sent to a shelter, where the network of beagle watchers alerted BREW. The group brought him to their adoption event, and he found a new owner. Shortly after adopting Roscoe, the new owner was hospitalized. From his hospital bed the owner organized some friends to feed and walk Roscoe, but Roscoe was increasingly frightened by the series of strangers and started relieving himself in the house. The owner called BREW, which took him back and boarded him at a kennel. While there he developed kennel cough, so he was transferred to a veterinary hospital for treatment.

After reading that, I needed a tranquilizer, so I couldn't imagine what kind of shape poor Roscoe was in. I picked up my daughter after school and we drove down to get him. When I first saw Roscoe he reminded me of a chimerical figure in Greek mythology, those half-lion, half-goat creatures. Roscoe had a small, brown beagle head, and a huge white, hoglike body decorated with black spots, as if someone had randomly glued 45 rpm records on him. Liberal affirmative action standards classified him as a beagle. He calmly walked to the car and got in the crate and didn't make a sound the entire ride back. When we got home I walked him around the block before taking him inside. It was clear he'd had no leash training. He pulled mightily, his nose on the ground, making snorting noises like a truffle pig on the hunt. It looked like he'd never been groomed nor had his nails clipped.

Then I brought him into the house. Sasha was thrilled and gnawed on his head in greeting, prompting both to chase each other around the first floor. After a few minutes of this, Roscoe came over in turn to me, my daughter, and husband, jumping up on us for a greeting. Sasha seemed confused and put out—why was her new friend paying attention to *people*? She came over and tried to egg on Roscoe to play, but he was too busy licking my husband. We gave Roscoe dinner and he ate his food slowly, interrupting his meal several times to come over to each of us, to thank us for the marvelous victuals. While we ate our dinner, he patiently sat under the dining room table, presenting himself as a footrest.

That night, when my husband went on evening guard duty—manning the television clicker while prone on the couch, Roscoe came bounding up on him, depositing himself with a thump on my husband's chest. Within minutes, he had shed an alpaca sweater's worth of white hair on my husband's navy sweatshirt. Roscoe stuck his head into my husband's neck and licked it furiously. From my perspective on the end of the couch, it looked like my husband was being given a hickey by someone the size of James Gandolfini. Then Roscoe feel asleep, head resting in my husband's armpit. My husband had his arm around Roscoe's midsection. They looked like they were on their honeymoon. However, I had been on my husband's honeymoon, and during it he hadn't looked that much in love.

"How do you like Roscoe?" I asked.

"I've never been so happy," my husband replied, a slight catch in his voice.

Although the cats slowly sidled into the den and took their places in the easy chair, Roscoe never acknowledged their presence. The next day we saw why Roscoe might have became a stray. He was casually walking around the house sniffing when he came upon Biscuit lying on the carpet. Roscoe immediately got down on his front paws, as if genuflecting before some terrible god, and began whining piteously. This aroused Biscuit's interest and he got up to inspect Roscoe, which only sent him into greater cries of terror. I had to come over, reassure Roscoe and lead him away.

I imagined Roscoe romping through the woods with his hunter who was training Roscoe to track rabbits. But when Roscoe saw one, he collapsed on the ground crying, "A bunny, a bunny. Help me, I'm scared!" Next, Roscoe and the hunter were driving through the woods in a pickup when the hunter swung open the door, gave Roscoe a shove, and kept on driving.

Roscoe was extremely quiet, so whenever I heard him whimpering, I knew I had to run and save him from an encounter with the cats. Other than that, Roscoe made himself at home. He discovered the basket of Sasha's toys in the den that sat mostly untouched. Sasha never figured out if she bit the head of the stuffed weasel it would squeak, but Roscoe did. Sasha never took to the plastic dinosaur chew toy, but Roscoe did. Each time Roscoe unearthed something, Sasha came over to try to wrestle it away from Roscoe, as if saying, "That's my very, very favorite. You can't play with that."

Walking the two dogs together made me feel the heartbreak of having a gorgeous child whom people fawned over and a homely one with a great personality whom everyone ignored. People would stop, lean down to pat Sasha and say, "What a beautiful beagle," then look at Roscoe and say, "What's that?"

Having Roscoe was both deflating and reassuring. Deflating because in one week we had gotten further in training Roscoe than we had in all our time with Sasha. For the same reason it was strangely reassuring. Despite the fact that most dog books blame dog problems on incompetent owners, Roscoe was proof that Sasha's deficiencies were not necessarily our fault. Roscoe did things unprecedented in our dog experience. For example, call out, "Roscoe!" and he immediately ran *to* you. Roscoe made a particular bond with my husband. When my husband came in the door at night, it was Roscoe who ran to greet him. While I was making dinner and my daughter was watching her television allotment, we heard the two of them wrestling in the front hall. "I love you, too, big boy, I love you, too," my husband said with a laugh, finally getting the kind of attention and affection he had hoped a wife and child would provide.

Roscoe moved me in a way I found disturbing. In the evening, when my husband, Roscoe, and I were on the couch, if I got up for any reason, Roscoe leapt off my husband to follow me. He seemed to be saying, "Everything okay? Need some company? I just want to be with you." Such behavior from another person would have you petitioning for a restraining order. But from Roscoe it felt like love. I had been led to believe love was based on knowing another deeply. I was just the new warm body who fed Roscoe—he couldn't really love me, could he? It didn't matter, because he tripped the switch in my wiring reserved for dog love. I now understood what dog people were so gaga about. When I wanted to feel good, all I needed was a dose of Roscoe.

If Roscoe was a people-dog, it was clearer than ever Sasha was a dog-dog. Having Roscoe around let her plumb the lower depths of this nature. Take the morning I let the two dogs out into the backyard. There was big Roscoe squatting, and there was little Sasha with her mouth open under his rear. It was like a grotesque parody of a teenager working in a soft-serve ice cream shop with her mouth under the chocolate spigot.

For BREW's Web site I wrote a description of Roscoe that made him sound like a combination of Lassie, Isaac Newton, and Rudolph Valentino. Laura told me that families were calling and competing for the right to meet him. I arranged to have the first couple in line come to our house one evening. They were young and sweet, the wife was three months pregnant, and as I went upstairs to get him, I told them they would just love him.

They were sitting on the couch in the living room when we came down. I said, "Roscoe, come meet the people who would like you to be their dog." Roscoe, who had greeted all our visitors with an enthusiastic jump and lick, looked at them, narrowed his eyes, and growled.

"Roscoe, what are you doing?" I said, trying to bring him over to the couple. Roscoe dropped to his haunches and started barking. Then he threw his head back and bayed. This dog was a genius! He was saying to me, "I'm done with strangers." We had been torn about giving Roscoe up, but I now realized he had more control over this situation than we did. Have someone sent by BREW arrive at the door and he turned himself into the hound of the Baskervilles.

The husband suggested that I get him some treats with which to entice Roscoe. I gave him a handful of dog food. Roscoe growled and snapped at his outstretched hand. I sat down next to Roscoe to calm him down and he practically knocked me over in his attempt to show that I was his woman.

I suggested that I bring down Sasha, hoping she would distract Roscoe from his new enemies. I let her out of her crate and she immediately bounded into the husband's arms and started begging for the treats. He fed them to her and she excitedly licked him. The wife got down on the floor next to her husband and Sasha began licking her. They both laughed and remarked on how adorable and friendly Sasha was. If they had decided to stand up, walk out the door, and go to their car, Sasha would have happily followed. Did a small voice inside me say, "They'd be so happy with Sasha and you'd be so happy with Roscoe"? Sure. But that's the same small voice that says to some White House residents, "That intern is *really* attracted to me." I realized, as I told the voice to shut up, that I loved Sasha even if she was no Roscoe.

After a few minutes Roscoe became intrigued with the love-fest between Sasha and the new couple and tentatively approached them. I praised him and he let them stroke him. In ten minutes, he was alternating between their laps. The wife said, "I like him."

That night I told my family this was the moment of truth. This couple might actually want Roscoe. We couldn't let this go any further if we wanted to keep him. I didn't want to end up as one of those Court TV cases in which two adoptive families fight for the same oblivious baby.

I called Laura that night to tell her about the visit, and I started making noises about how much we liked Roscoe. She immediately said, "Tell me you don't want to adopt him, please. If you take Roscoe you're helping one dog. If you remain a foster family you can help many, many dogs."

I faced my family: "Do we want to keep him?"

"Mom, we made an agreement," my daughter said. "I think we have to let another family adopt Roscoe." I was stunned at her maturity. Then it occurred to me—she's jealous! Sasha was the adorable but incorrigible younger sister who was always getting in trouble. Roscoe was the brother who got endless praise and attention from the parents.

The next day I got an e-mail from Laura saying the couple wanted Roscoe. We made arrangements for them to pick him up the following Saturday. My husband couldn't stand it. He took our daughter shopping and left me to bid adieu.

When they arrived at the door Roscoe barked for a few minutes, then he let them bend down and stroke him. I took a minute alone with him. "Good-bye, big boy. You have a new family who will love you as much as we do." The husband put a leash on Roscoe and they went down the front stairs. I watched through the glass in the front door as they walked him up and down the block for a few minutes. Then they led him to their car and opened the crate in the backseat. As they tugged on the leash to try to get him to go in, Roscoe turned and quizzically looked up at our front door. Then he followed their commands and got in the car.

That night, as my husband lay on the couch, bereft, Sasha came into the den and sat near his feet. "Come here, Sasha, come up and lie by me," my husband said, patting his chest. At the sound of the words "Sasha" and "come," Sasha got up and ran from the room.

11

CANINE 9II

"That dog saved my life."

One day as I was walking Sasha, my neighbor Heidi patted Sasha's head and sighed that she wished her family's work schedule allowed having a dog. She had loved growing up with them. "One of my dogs saved my life," she said.

"How?" I asked.

Heidi was eight and her parents decided she was ready for a dog. They took her to the local shelter where Heidi saw a tiny terrier mix, already on the executioner's schedule. The dog was fifteen pounds of quivering, matted fur. She was three years old and had been abused by her previous owners, a big selling point for Heidi's mother, who had a strong missionary streak. They brought the dog home, bathed her, and saw that she had a lovely, light brown coat. Heidi named the dog Honey. "For the first three weeks she hid under the dining room table," said Heidi. "She'd jump if I tried to touch her." Heidi was precociously patient and sat at the edge of the table, over weeks gradually moving into petting range. Eventually Honey allowed herself to be touched.

Although Honey remained shy around strange people and animals, she and Heidi were deeply attached. Heidi's family was living in rural Virginia and Honey became Heidi's companion on her wanderings.

That summer Heidi, her parents, and Honey went on a four-day camping trip to Shenandoah National Park. On the final day of the trip Heidi's parents left her at the campsite while they returned their gear to the car, about a quarter mile away. While Heidi looked for bugs and jumped off rocks, Honey followed along. Suddenly the brush at the edge of their campsite rustled, and as if making a nervous debut on stage, a bear cub stumbled into the clearing in front of Heidi.

"I remember thinking that it was a stuffed animal come to life," Heidi recalled. "It was a real, live baby and I was soaking it in." Heidi was captivated by the shiny little nose and paws, and she moved in to touch. "Honey was a few feet away and she gave me such a look," said Heidi.

Heidi was not about to be deterred by a dubious glance from a terrier, so she continued toward the bear. The cub seemed just as curious about Heidi and ambled toward her. Heidi was just reaching out her hand when there was a crashing noise from the spot where the cub had emerged. The brambles shook again, and this time into the opening came the cub's mother.

Heidi didn't even look at Honey—she didn't need an "I told you so" from her dog. Heidi was terrified by the massive black-coated mother. The mother immediately understood Heidi had designs on her baby, and snapped her jaws, displaying her long, pointed teeth. Heidi thought this would be an opportune time for her own mother to show up and take her back to to the car. When she didn't, Heidi took a few steps toward the path. The bear deftly moved to block Heidi's way.

Then the bear got up on her hind legs, waved her paws, and

roared. An average black mother bear weighs two hundred pounds and stands at five feet. Heidi's thoughts consisted of, "Those claws! Those teeth! Where's my mom!"

She stood frozen, the angry mother bear threatening her, when she suddenly became aware of another angry animal. Honey was now at her side. Facing the bear, Honey got up on her own hind legs. She stood at just over a foot. She too pawed the air, then let out a half-strangled growl. The bear, still on her haunches, looked down at Honey. The bear's expression was obvious: "What is *that*?" Again Honey waved the air and let out her strange choking sound. The bear stared at Honey, and Honey pawed the air. Finally, with a thud, the bear dropped down on all fours, nudged her cub, and the two disappeared back into the brambles.

At that moment Honey sprinted up the trail toward the parking lot. "I was running, too, but I couldn't keep up with her," said Heidi. Without a moment's hesitation Honey found the family car and stopped at its rear hubcap. She opened her mouth and let loose a jet of projectile vomit. She vomited until she couldn't stand, then collapsed like a deflated balloon. Heidi told her parents what had happened. Her parents quickly finished packing the car. They didn't take their usual one last look at the campsite to make sure they hadn't left anything behind. Honey rode home on Heidi's mother's lap, unconscious.

While Honey discovered she had greatness in her, there are some dogs whose reason for being is to save lives. Joan, a potter who lives in rural Vermont, had Newfoundlands who felt this way. Newfoundlands are huge, thick-coated dogs who love the water. *The International Encyclopedia of Dogs* writes this is well illustrated by nineteenth-century artist Edwin Landseer's portrait of a Newfoundland titled *Saved* in which the dog is hovering over a little girl he has just rescued from drowning. That dog was obviously the ancestor of Joan's Newfoundland Abigail. "She would rescue people who were swimming, even if they didn't want to be," Joan recalled. All summer long, as children splashed in the nearby pond, Abigail would with great seriousness follow them in, gently take their wrist in her mouth, and pull them to shore.

Another of her Newfoundlands, Caesar, did actually rescue someone in need. Joan's mother, a tiny, delicate woman in her seventies, had come to visit. She was staying in the guesthouse a little down the road. Joan's mother woke up earlier than everyone else and before breakfast liked to take a walk. As she set off one dawn, the family's new goat, Delilah, approached her.

Delilah was actually a foster goat, belonging to the family on a neighboring farm. Joan's family agreed to take her temporarily after her real owner threatened bodily harm to Delilah for eating all his newly planted fruit trees. "Delilah was nasty," recalled Joan. "She was big, and white and beautiful, like a unicorn without the horn. But she didn't like anybody except Caesar, whom she adored and would follow everywhere." Delilah, who was the goat version of the Glenn Close character in *Fatal Attraction*, particularly hated the other Newfoundland, Abigail, a competitor for Caesar's attentions.

Since Delilah had nothing better to do, when she saw Joan's mother, she decided to knock her down. When the elderly woman tried to scramble to her feet, Delilah again came at her headfirst. It could have been a commercial for a medical alert system: "Help, I'm being butted by a goat and I can't get up!" Joan's mother's cries went unheard by everyone. Except Caesar. As soon as he picked up the feeble calls, the huge dog came bounding over the hill. He quickly assessed the situation, then started barking ferociously at Delilah. Since Caesar's opinion was the only one Delilah cared about, the goat retreated. "My mother had never been a dog fan," said Joan. "But she was devoted to Caesar for the rest of her life."

*   *   *

I discovered I had yet another friend with a lifesaving dog. This came up at brunch at Cindy's house, when she started telling stories about her Lhasa apso, Cinnamon. Cinnamon was born to be the center of attention. After we ate, she went from guest to guest, allowing each of us to place her on our lap and stroke her mop of tan fur.

The decision to get a dog was a years-long process. From the time Cindy's daughter, Maddie, was two years old, she started lobbying for a brother or sister (this was starting to sound familiar to me).

"When we finally convinced her that wasn't going to happen, she started begging for a dog or a cat," Cindy said. Cindy's husband, Bruce, is allergic to both animals, and when Maddie was three, Cindy explained that to her. "Mommy, I just had an idea," Maddie replied. "We could get a kitten and Dad could move out." Because Bruce was less allergic to cats, when Maddie turned six, they got a kitten, and Bruce got a basket of inhalers and pills. Their cat was a bust—aloof, hissing, and scratching—so Maddie soon started asking for a dog. As a tactic to stop the begging, Cindy said Maddie could get one when she was ten.

Maddie stopped talking about dogs for the following three years. On her ninth birthday she told her mother they had one year to go until they got a dog. When she turned ten, she started reading the "Dogs for Sale" section of the newspaper. Cindy was driving home from visiting her parents in Pennsylvania when her cell phone rang. Maddie had just seen an ad for Lhasa apsos in Harper's Ferry, about an hour's detour from Cindy's drive. Cindy was five minutes from the exit and she took it. She got to the breeder's house and looked over the eight puppies, picked the most laid-back one, and put it on the front seat.

"I love this dog," Cindy said, pointing to the sleeping mop. "I want to cuddle her every second."

Cindy is a travel writer and two weeks after she got Cinnamon she went on assignment to Gettysburg. She and Maddie had planned to go together, but they couldn't bear to leave Cinnamon, who was so tiny Cindy could hold her in one hand. Taking Cinnamon would also give Bruce a break. He'd recently had to add weekly allergy shots to the regimen that allowed him to breathe in his own home. Cindy found a bed and breakfast out in the country where dogs were welcome.

They left late on Friday, stopped to pick up dinner on the way, and arrived around eleven P.M. Cindy and Maddie sat down at the dining room table and were eating their sandwiches when Maddie said, "Mom, Cinnamon is playing with a huge bug!" Cindy looked down and saw her puppy was chasing a mouse.

"I grabbed the mouse from her and took it outside," said Cindy. "It was hurt but still alive. I had to put it out of its misery so I stomped it between two pieces of newspaper."

Cindy disposed of the mouse and went inside to find Cinnamon playing with a buddy of the recently deceased. She took the second injured mouse outside and dispatched it. Upon her return, Cinnamon was at work on a third mouse. "By this point I was shaking," said Cindy. (Okay, okay, this is a story about a life-saving dog who starts out as a mouse-killing dog.) It was midnight, but she and Maddie decided to pack it in. They grabbed Cinnamon and knocked on the owner's door.

She came out in her bathrobe and Cindy explained their room was infested with mice.

"I'll give you a glue trap," said the proprietor.

Cindy envisioned waking up to several mice quivering on the glue trap and Cinnamon stuck to it by her tongue.

"We have to go," said Cindy.

"This is the country, I don't know what you expect," huffed the woman.

They left. They looked at the cheap highway motels ringing the city but all of them were full. Finally, they arrived in historic downtown, at the most expensive hotel in Gettysburg. Cindy went up the desk clerk and explained her dilemma.

"I wish you hadn't told me you had a dog because I could have given you a room," said the clerk. "But now that I know, I have to refuse you."

Cindy went back to the car, waited ten minutes, then went back inside.

"I found a kennel," she said. "It's just my daughter and me."

"You did not," said the clerk.

"Yes I did," said Cindy.

She got the room. Cindy parked around back. Maddie went through the lobby then opened the back door. Cindy stuck Cinnamon under her sweatshirt and they went to their room. They put Cinnamon in the bathroom with newspapers on the floor and they all went to sleep. The next morning Cindy put Cinnamon back in her sweatshirt to sneak her to the car so she and Maddie could get breakfast. When the elevator stopped a hotel employee got on and eyed Cindy suspiciously. Finally she spoke.

"You have a dog with you," she said.

"No I don't," said Cindy.

"Then why is a leash hanging out of your sweatshirt?"

Cindy and Maddie decided to skip breakfast and leave.

As Cindy told the story, Cinnamon stared at her intently. Cinnamon had had enough of hearing about her embarrassing childhood escapades and clearly wanted Cindy to tell about her heroics.

Cindy's living room is on the second story, and has a huge picture window overlooking the neighborhood and the hills beyond. Cinnamon loves to get on a chair and look out the window, monitoring neighborhood activity. "She'll bark if she sees a stranger, and I'll go to her and reassure her it's okay," said Cindy.

It was late one night in January and the president had just given the State of the Union address. Bruce, who is a reporter, was calling senators to get their reaction for a story he had to file immediately. But while he was doing his interviews, Cinnamon, in position by the window, started barking. Bruce signaled to Cindy to make the dog shut up. Cindy went over to Cinnamon, looked outside and saw nothing—no neighbors, no strangers, no dogs. "Cinnamon, it's okay, be quiet." But Cinnamon stared down the street and increased her barking. Cindy dragged her from the window, but Cinnamon ran back up and started barking again. Cindy hit her with a rolled-up newspaper ("I felt so terrible," she said) but Cinnamon kept barking.

Finally, Cindy stood next to Cinnamon and looked in the direction she was looking. "I saw smoke and a wisp of fire coming out of the house across the street and a few doors down," said Cindy. She got Bruce off the phone and called the fire department. She went out and knocked on the door of the house but there was no answer. She went to a neighbor, who said the house was occupied by an elderly woman who was hard of hearing. By this time flames were lapping from the house. The neighbor called the woman's son.

As they were standing there, waiting for the fire department, KA-BOOM. "The carport, the car parked in it, and the deck blew up," said Cindy. Seconds later the firemen arrived. As they did, the woman opened the door to the burning side of the house. The firefighters screamed at her to close it—she was about to immolate herself. They went in through the front door and rescued her.

If it hadn't been for Cinnamon's warning, the first anyone would have known of the impending disaster would have been the explosion, the woman would have walked right into it, and the house would soon have been engulfed. "The firemen said if they hadn't gotten there right when they did, the woman would have died," said Cindy.

We all praised Cinnamon who was now modestly asleep on my husband's lap.

The only way I could see Sasha saving someone's life was if she jumped up on the dining room table and ate a hamburger that was later revealed to have come from a mad cow.

12

MADAME BUTTERFLY

Our next foster, Maggie.

Within days of Roscoe's departure, I got an e-mail from BREW saying they had the perfect dog to be our next foster: Maggie. Again, I went to the Web site. "Maggie is an ex-hunting dog who was hit by a car. Her leg was broken, but a good Samaritan took her in and got her all fixed up. Now, her leg is totally healed, she's spayed and current on shots." Maggie had been living at the good Samaritan's town house with two kids, a Labrador, and a cat, until the good Samaritan realized he was a living demonstration of the phrase "No good deed goes unpunished," and passed Maggie on to BREW.

I drove to the veterinarian's office an hour away where Maggie was boarding. She was about thirty pounds with small, sad, downturned eyes, extra-long ears, and a copper and black coat. She too rode silently all the way home. I arrived at our house at nine-thirty P.M. and, before bringing her in, took her to relieve her bladder. She was such a focused scent hound, that she walked around our block as if she was reading a novel in Braille with her nose. By ten-twenty I had discovered alleys in my neighborhood I'd never seen before, and Maggie hadn't even made a feint at squatting. I went inside. Maggie came in the door, then turned over on her back in the front hall, eyes closes, legs splayed, begging to be stroked. Sasha came running over, inspected Maggie, then tried to bark her into an upright position. Maggie opened her eyes, glanced at Sasha, then closed her eyes and turned her head. My husband and I got down on the floor and stroked and reassured her. She had enormous pink nipples, like two rows of foam earplugs, and rubbing our hands along her chest was bizarrely intimate. She must have felt that way, too, because she soon started emitting birdlike cheeps of pleasure, while looking at us with her sad, downturned eyes.

If Roscoe was the Barney of beagles ("I love you, you love me"), Maggie was the Madame Butterfly, hoping—against all experience—that she will find love. Sitting on the floor with her, I noticed a couple of things. One, that her long velvet ears were ragged and scarred. I imagined her being caught in brambles and barbed wire, as some guy with a shotgun cursed at her. Two, she had a distinct aroma—something in the cheese family. The kind of cheese the French age in caves until it's so aromatic that only people with great sophistication, or chronic sinus infection, can eat it.

"Let's give her a bath," I said to my husband.

We took her to the bathroom and immediately she sat down on the mat and emptied a bladder that must have been the size of a gasoline can. We put her in the tub. Sasha usually tried to escape during a bath, but Maggie was as implacable as a guard at Buckingham Palace. The bath was not an unmitigated success. She now smelled like French cheese served on wet-dog crackers. At her request, we gave her another nipple massage, then put her in the crate.

We were used to dogs shooting out of their crates in the morning. But Maggie slithered out on her back, legs splayed. Again we rubbed her nipples and she emitted little love arias. After a few minutes we stood up, but Maggie stayed in place, in an alpha-wave state so deep she could teach transcendental meditation.

"This is so cool," said my daughter. "She looks like she's dead!"

We prodded Maggie back to life and I took her into our back-yard. She and Sasha played with each other for twenty minutes, sufficient time for the first urination of the day.

Back inside she ate calmly and explored the house. Then she encountered the cats. Immediately she fell into what we started calling her backstroke. The cats too were fascinated by her nip-ples. They tried to inconspicuously sidle up to Maggie, then sent out a paw to snag a nipple, like catching a guppy in an aquarium. Maggie took it for a while, then rolled over onto her belly and shooed them away. We understood why Maggie, like Roscoe, was a former hunting dog. If she fell into a swoon every time she saw a rabbit, we could imagine her hunter, door to the pickup thrown open, pushing her into her new fate with a farewell of, "Get out, you moron."

We quickly grew fond of Maggie. A fondness that was tem-pered the night we were putting our daughter to bed and she said as she got under the covers, "Why is my bed all wet?" It turned out that Maggie too was a bed wetter. Then we found her on our own bed one night lying in her puddle. I took Todd's dictum to heart and had her spend more time in her crate. Getting her in it was like shoving a giant calzone into the oven. But Maggie was calm and gentle, and we felt we could help her shed her tragic view of the world.

I wrote up her personal ad for the BREW Web site, empha-sizing her serene nature, and the scars of the cruel past she still bore on her long, soft ears. I knew this detail was a killer, and sure enough, families were soon lining up. I didn't mention her ineradicable odor, or our soggy-mattress problem. Those were minor issues, I thought, compared with Maggie's sterling qualities. I wasn't just a dog person, now I was practically a dogist.

A couple eager to meet Maggie soon called. It turned out this wife too was three months pregnant, with twins, no less. BREW's Web site regularly features beagles that are being given away because the owners are going to have a baby and don't want a dog anymore. I was encountering the other pole of humanity. These were the couples, upon discovering they are going to become parents, who don't have the patience to wait for the baby to finish gestating. They've got to have something to cuddle right now. Maggie behaved beautifully with this couple, stretching across their laps to be petted. The wife stroked her ears, then inspected their ragged bottoms. "Oh, look at what she's been through!" she said, while Maggie emitted some chirps. I knew the adoption would soon be sealed.

They came a few days later to pick up Maggie. We sat and talked about Maggie while she and Sasha wrestled upstairs. I brought Maggie down and we all gave her a sad hug good-bye and final nipple rub. Then I went to our bedroom and noticed our white comforter had a Lake Erie–sized yellow puddle on the end of it. As the saying goes, "Pee on my bed once, shame on you. Pee on my bed twenty-seven times, you're a beagle."

After Maggie left we were expecting a series of houseguests. I told Laura I needed a few weeks to air out the mattresses before we took on another foster. I was curious how both Roscoe and Maggie were doing at their new homes, so I sent e-mails to their owners. Roscoe's father sent a note saying, "He's a good boy and we love him. He's been a great blessing to us." He attached a picture of the two of them frolicking in the grass. I didn't have the heart to let my husband see it.

Maggie had become Cooper and was, according to her happy new owners, just as we had described her, except that from the time they brought her home she had been completely housebroken. I found this last bit of information hard to take. Had Maggie, ah, Cooper thought, "Well, the mattress peeing was fun while it lasted, but now it's time to shape up?" I consoled myself that somewhere in a corner of Cooper's new home was a piece of rug pad moldering with urine.

13

VOYAGE OF THE BEAGLE

Sasha is evolving into a real pet.

Nothing told me how much I'd changed since getting Sasha than finding myself at the annual holiday party of friends where I first mentioned a year earlier that I was being pressured to get a dog. I was talking to the wife of one of the antidog couples, who had futilely told me to stand firm against my family's lobbying. This year she said that a bunch of their friends had just gotten dogs.

"It's incredible, their lives are completely turned upside down," she said.

I nodded.

"We were trying to make plans with one of them to do something with the kids and the wife said they couldn't be away from the house for more than five hours," my friend said incredulously.

I immediately thought, Five whole hours, that's pretty good!

"You don't live like that, do you?" my friend said.

Fortunately, before I could answer the host offered to freshen up our drinks and the subject changed.

The more amazing part was that I didn't resent it anymore.

Instead, when I had to be away for longer than five hours, my thought was, "Poor Sasha. I've got to make this up to her."

Sasha was becoming fun. She liked to jump on our bed while my husband was reading and show her belly so he would roughhouse with her. When they got going she let out the most unearthly growl, a long cry that sounded as if she was saying, "Ahhh-rahhh-nahhh, ahh-rahh-nahhh!!!!" After a few minutes of ah-rah-nah, she got so overwhelmed with the pleasure of it that she ran and hid in her crate, like a high school student who had taken a vow of abstinence fleeing from a spin-the-bottle party. Then her desire got the better of her and she'd run back to the bed, and present her belly again.

Although we had reached a new level in our relationship with Sasha, we could never forget she was a beagle. She was constantly lifting the lid on the kitchen garbage can, spreading the contents all over the house, and hoarding the choicest bits in her crate. I spent months searching for a garbage can that would defeat her. When I finally found it, I realized my wedding day, the birth of my daughter, and the purchase of my garbage can were the three happiest days of my life.

While we were thoroughly warned by BREW that a beagle can never be let off-leash, after you've had a beagle for a while you start to think that she'll appreciate the deal she has with you. You convince yourself that even if the opportunity arises, she's not going to take off like a maniac, head for the Atlantic Ocean, and try to make it across so she can search for members of the royal family who still appreciate beagles. This is an incorrect assumption. Even if you fed your beagle an organic chicken breast an hour ago, if the fence is unlocked, she's heading for the *QEII*.

I discovered this one evening when the doorbell rang while I was making dinner. I had put Sasha into the backyard a short time before. She'd been confined to the house all day because a painter had been working out back. I almost didn't go to the door, figuring it was someone with a petition, but on the second insistent ring I went. There was a strange man standing there. In his left hand were two leashes, each attached to a huge, hairy black dog. Around each dog's thick neck was a chain-link collar tipped with inward-facing half-inch-long spikes. In the man's right arm was Sasha. Sasha was lolling in a kind of swoon. The look on her face said, "Oh, mercy me. How did I ever end up in this S&M parlor with two such brutes? What are your names again, boys?"

I had discussed with Todd Sasha's propensity to run at the first opportunity. How, after she'd escaped, I'd spot her chewing on the carcass of some West Nile–infected crow and sneak up on her, only to have her bolt at the sight of me.

"What do you do when you finally get her?" he asked.

"I say, 'Bad dog.'"

"Does that make sense? When she finally does what you want— allow herself to be caught—you punish her. In her mind the bad thing she's doing is letting you get her. If she escapes that's because *you've* made a mistake. When she finally comes to you, even it if it's involuntarily, you should praise her." I often wondered if Todd's combination of wisdom and common sense came from his close observation of the kooky behavior of dogs or of their owners.

It turned out the painter had closed, but not latched, the fence. I thanked the man, who complimented me on Sasha's good looks as I took her from his arms. She had only been gone a few minutes, but when he saw her sitting at the corner, it was apparent she was a lost dog. That showed how different today's canine world was from the one I grew up in. Back then no one would have noticed an unleashed dog unless it was in the last stages of rabies, like Old Yeller.

Dogs had the day to themselves, then came home for dinner.

It wasn't that different for children. I started walking to school by myself at age five, and sometimes took long, roundabout detours on the half-mile-long trip home. In my neighborhood now, seeing a free-roaming child is as unlikely as a free-roaming dog. I want my daughter's whereabouts constantly accounted for, but I also know that she's lost something by not being able to decide to take a turn down a different block and see what's there. Sasha is safer too, at the end of my arm, but I understand her desire to throw off civilization and go out and roll in something smelly.

Of course, there were plenty of smelly things right in our house. Once my daughter was having one of her friends over, and I heard him yell, "Sasha got a diaper, Sasha got a diaper!" I ran to my daughter's room where Sasha was in her crate tearing apart a used sanitary napkin. The children were staring into the crate. I put my hand in and tried to gather up the stuffing while Sasha fought for her trophy. "It's a very weird diaper," the friend said. "It's got blood on it." Then he looked at me like a prepubscent Sherlock Holmes. "And you don't even have a baby. How come you have weird diapers?" I decided to take the non sequitur approach to this.

"Ha, ha, ha, that Sasha is always playing!" I said, as I fled the room.

Most of my daughter's friends loved Sasha. She was well known among them because I took Sasha with me when I walked to school to pick up my daughter. I thought Sasha would even be part of the entertainment for my daughter's seventh birthday. We had agreed to a sleepover party, with a guest list of four girls. My doubts about this enterprise grew as each parent in turn dropped off a daughter and said, "Wow, you're brave. Now here's my cell phone number, and my pager, don't worry about calling too late if you need to . . ."

Then Sophia arrived, and Sasha enthusiastically came to greet her. Sophia jumped into her father's arms, sobbing. "I hate dogs, I hate dogs. Get it away, get it away." My husband and I looked at each other—why hadn't we insisted on a bowling party?

Sophia's father tried to show her how little and cute Sasha was, but Sophia was too blinded by tears. I put Sasha out back and promised Sophia she would stay outside until the girls went to bed, then we would keep her in our bedroom. "I don't want any dogs in the house!" Sophia screamed. Her father convinced her that we would keep the dog away from her, but that Sophia couldn't insist we get rid of the dog. Dubiously, Sophia bid her father farewell.

We got through the hide-and-seek, the treasure hunt, the pizza, the birthday cake, and the movie and now it was time for bed. I was getting concerned about Sasha. We had set up a pile of blankets for her in the garage, but this was December, and it was cold. Around ten P.M. we got the girls settled down, all except one who announced the start of a "Let's stay up all night" contest and began jumping on the mattresses. When her father came to retrieve her at eleven forty-five, the remaining three girls quickly drifted off to sleep. At twelve-fifteen we let Sasha in. We had taken her crate out of its usual place in our daughter's room and put it in our room—but we were going to allow her to sleep on our bed, anyway. "Come on, Sasha, come see Daddy," I said, leading her to our bedroom. But instead of jumping on our bed, as she did every night, she immediately made a turn for my daughter's room. I suddenly realized the funk of four small, sweaty, pizza- and cake-covered bodies trumped our bed.

Naturally, Sasha pounced on the ripest target—Sophia. Before I could even get in the room, I heard her neighbor-waking scream. I opened the door to see Sasha sitting squarely on Sophia's chest, her snout pressed deeply into Sophia's face, licking madly. Even a dog lover might be disturbed to be awakened in such a manner. Looking at Sophia and Sasha, I was reminded of the scene in George Orwell's *1984* in which disobedient citizens are hauled away and sent to room 101. There they are confronted with individually tailored torture based on their deepest dreads. I picked up Sasha, who extended her tongue for one last lick.

"You can stop screaming now, Sophia," I said. "I'm holding Sasha."

Sophia looked up at me, her dark eyes burning, "I'm going crazy in here!" she shrieked.

I now had four wide-awake girls.

My daughter was next. "I need a Tylenol right now!" she screamed. I was taken aback since we never called acetaminophen by its brand name.

The other two girls, less melodramatically, observed that it was very hard to sleep when people in the room were yelling. I hustled Sasha to our bedroom, where as a precautionary measure I put her in her crate, and returned to the scene of the assault.

Sophia settled down to the level of gasping, but tearless, sobs. "You promised me the dog wouldn't bother me and she was sitting on me and she was licking me!"

"Well, that must mean you're the sweetest one," I said, prompting the observation from our other guests that they felt they were far sweeter than Sophia. My daughter, as if we had fast-forwarded eighty years to the nursing home, again demanded immediate medication: "Where's my Tylenol!"

Finally, exhaustion kicked in and all four drifted back to sleep. I kept Sasha contained until Sophia's mother came to retrieve her in the morning. I wanted to pull the mother aside and warn her about nightmares and room 101, but there was no opportunity. The next day at school, I saw the mother again, and just as I was about to apologize, Sophia's mother said, "I can't thank you enough for having Sophia over. She spent the rest of the day talking about how that was the best party she'd ever been to." I told this to my husband, but it didn't shake our conviction that we would celebrate our daughter's eighth birthday at the bowling alley.

14

AN AMERICAN GENTLEMAN (OR WOMAN)

Trying to get a Boston terrier into my life.

Since our foster efforts had worked out so well, I decided the foster route might be the way to go to get a Boston terrier into my life. Why not have a series of Bostons? I admit I spent too much time cruising Boston terrier sites, imagining one of the little bug-eyed, tuxedoed dogs was mine. Often I did this while Sasha was sleeping under my desk. I did feel a little like a husband who announces he's going on the Internet to investigate refinancing the house, and instead joins the "I love to wear tutus" chat room.

The opportunity to make my pitch came when I saw on the American Kennel Club Web site that the national Boston terrier championships were being held at a conference center about an hour away, and that the local Boston terrier rescue organization was going to have a booth there. I figured that by showing up and filling out an application I would impress them with my love of the breed.

Trailers with license plates from around the country filled the parking lot. Next to them impromptu kennels had been set up.

One van had a vanity plate, AM-GENTS, for "American Gentleman." Then, as if a director had yelled "Action!" half a dozen Boston terriers started prancing across the tarmac with their owners. I felt disoriented, as if I were in a recurring childhood dream in which I opened my bedroom closet to find it's the entrance to F.A.O. Schwarz.

I walked around to a field in the back of the hotel where the agility trials were taking place. The small sets of rings and bars strategically placed on the grass looked like a military obstacle course for lilliputians. The judge called out a number and a woman picked up her Boston and carried it to the starting line. She took off its leash and stood just past the first set of rings and said, "Come, Vicki." Boston terriers are compact but full-chested. The adorable Vicki resembled a large turkey leg jumping through the rings.

I went inside where the rest of the competition was being held. Hanging over one of the first tables ringing the room was a banner that read BOSTON TERRIER RESCUE SAVING THE AMERICAN GENTLEMAN. My heart lurched at the thought that somewhere my American gentleman or woman was waiting for me. I went over to the table and introduced myself to the man sitting behind it. I said I was the person who had left a phone message saying I was coming to the show and that I hoped to be a foster parent.

"You need to talk to my wife, Sylvie, she's the one who handles this. I'm just sitting here." He said his name was Paul and that Sylvie would be back shortly. While I waited Paul and I got into a conversation about the dogs. Paul told me that he and Sylvie lived in a town house and that it was not unusual for them to have twelve Boston terrier fosters. I asked him if the neighbors objected.

"We walk them two at a time," he said. "They're all black-and-white, so the neighbors think we only have two dogs." He explained they usually had that many because Sylvie was extremely picky who she let foster or adopt the dogs. I tried to ask more questions, but Paul seemed exhausted by the topic.

"You need to talk to Sylvie. I'm not even a member of the organization because I don't want anything to do with it." Yes, Paul, I thought, you've done as good a job separating yourself from Boston terriers as Carmela Soprano has separating herself from the mob. Then Paul saw Sylvie across the room and sent me over to her.

She was a tiny woman holding a fairly big Boston terrier. She said she'd gotten my message but had been very busy lately with various dog and family responsibilities. She then put her dog's leash in my hand. "Hold Mikey while I get an application for you." I bent down to pat Mikey. He turned to face me and calmly regarded me with one large brown eye. The other socket was sewn shut. When Sylvie returned I asked what had happened to Mikey's eye.

"He had an accident," she said, clearly closing the subject. I asked her how she got into Boston rescue.

She had been doing mixed-breed rescue for years. She would take a dog from the shelter, train it, then give it to a good family. Then she got a dog that hated kids, and she had three of them, and she decided she'd had enough with shelter dogs. Her mother suggested she try purebreds, in particular Boston terriers. Like many people of a certain age, Sylvie's mother had had a Boston as a child when they were the fashionable dog of the day. Sylvie immediately fell in love with the breed. "They don't know they're dogs. They think they're little humans." Like little humans, she said, "If they don't feel like doing something, they won't."

Sylvie pointed out people around the room who had rescued Bostons. "That lady has a rescue," she said. "Like a lot of Bostons, it only has one eye." Since she brought it up, I asked why Mikey had univision.

"He was living with a German shorthaired pointer. It smacked him on the back of the head a million times. But on this particular occasion Mikey's eye came out."

I was going to say, "I see," but thought better of it. Sylvie told me she didn't have any fosters available, but would contact me when she got one that might fit in with my household. I was thinking, "Make it one with really tight sockets."

I wandered off to look at the tables of sale items. There were Boston pins and earrings and necklaces. Boston postcards and stationery. Boston stuffed animals. Boston totes and vests. There was a huge rug portraying many Bostons sitting solemnly around a table; maybe it was meant to be a Boston *Last Supper*. One large woman, with a tiny Boston at the end of a leash, was examining the clothing table. After a few minutes she walked away, saying to her dog, "Mamma needs another T-shirt like she needs another bitch in heat." Another woman stopped at the table. Her Boston was in a baby carrier slung across her back.

The obedience competition was beginning. An official took the microphone to call everybody to order and to play a tape of "The Star-Spangled Banner." "Let us remember our brave soldiers overseas," she said, "who allow us to be free and enjoy dog sports." I wondered how many of our brave soldiers, upon hearing sniper fire, gathered the strength to face the enemy by taking one last look at a photo, hanging from a dog tag, of a Boston terrier jumping through an agility hoop.

After the national anthem I sat down next to a middle-aged woman wearing a shirt with a Boston embroidered on the breast pocket and a watch with a Boston on the face. In the ring a woman in her seventies—it was clear that Bostons are primarily a woman's dog—screamed, "Rollie, SIT!" I don't know anything about dog shows, but my impression was that when you scream, "SIT" your dog is not supposed to stroll away. Rollie kept strolling and finally the woman picked him up and left the ring, muttering, "He's lost his interest."

Another owner placed her dog at one end of the ring then walked to the other side. She called, "Sissy, come." Sissy, like many of the dogs, had skinny, fast legs, which gave her an insect-like quality. Sissy started walking to her owner then halfway across stopped and began scratching her ear with her hind leg. She scratched and scratched, then slowly got up and made it across the ring. The owner said, "Sissy, down." Sissy continued standing and gave her owner an oblivious look.

I had two thoughts. One, as a demonstration of obedience, this stinks. Two, maybe Sasha could compete.

Next, a woman told her dog to get down, which he did. Then she said, "Stay." She turned her back and walked to the end of the ring, and kept walking. She left the ring and the room. I saw her disappear into the public bathroom, which had taped to the door a sign with a drawing of a Boston and a slash through it and the words PLEASE. NO BOSTONS IN RESTROOM.

Everyone sat silently. The dog looked around forlornly, like a child who always gets separated from his mother at the department store. He seemed anxious, yet resigned. I asked the woman next to me what was going on. "It's called a 'long down.' The dog is supposed to stay in place for five minutes." Finally the owner returned to great applause.

Next came Charlie. His owner said, "Heel, Charlie," at which Charlie made a break for the opening to the ring. Two officials pounced on him and returned him to his owner. A woman near me said, "Charlie ain't doing too sharp here." I was grateful I wasn't the only one concluding the competition was becoming farcical. I wondered if everyone was having an off day or if Boston terriers are an off breed. Do most owners share the delusion that their dog can follow a command, the way most first-round competitors on *American Idol* share the delusion that they can carry a tune?

The judge called a number and the last couple entered—an elderly lady who left her cane resting on her chair, and her dog, Christie. The woman limped heavily into the ring and the judge said to her and Christie, "Run." Run? Was this guy a sadist? The woman and Christie were supposed to run together. Christie trotted along, but the woman lumbered, at one point throwing out her arms for balance, prompting the judge to grab her hand to steady her. The audience gasped. The two finally made it to the other side of the ring. The judge looked at them and said, "Run." Maybe he was an orthopedic surgeon looking for clients. The audience held its breath, hoping they made it back across the ring without the owner falling and turning her hip into streusel. When they both arrived we all sighed and clapped

The judge told the woman to cross the ring and call the dog. "Christie, come!" she shouted. Christie looked right and left. "To me!" the woman screamed. Christie sat where she was.

Finally, the judge called all three competitors into the ring. Charlie made another break for it and was again tackled by officials as if he was a football that had sprouted legs. He was returned to his owner and the judge spoke. He explained that everyone was after a green ribbon and to get one, the dogs had to get 170 points out of 200 and do 50 percent of the exercises correctly. "Today we didn't have any qualifiers," he said to a round of "Awwws" from the crowd. "In each case we had dogs who were close, but not quite. Close counts in horseshoes, hand grenades, and atomic bombs. But not obedience."

I got up and went to talk to a young mother with her five-year-old son in tow. She said that she and her mother-in-law jointly raised Bostons, although from different locales. Her mother-in-law had eight in a kennel in Pennsylvania and she had one at her home in Florida. Like all Boston owners, the woman praised the breed's gentleness and her son chimed in, "They lick my toes."

The woman explained her Boston had to be separated from the Pennsylvania pack because it became hostile to its mother. "She wanted to be the alpha dog and ripped her mother's eye out, so now the mother can't compete anymore. Her socket was sewn shut."

"One dog goes in when the other dog goes out," the five-year-old elaborated.

Again, I realized "I see" was not the right response.

Feeling a little watery in the knees, I wandered off. A woman with a Boston tattooed on her ankle caught my eye. I introduced myself and asked her how she got interested in Bostons. Her name was Cindy and she said that she'd always been a dog lover, and for years she raised Dobermans. Her neighbor had a Boston but she never cared for the breed until the neighbor gave her one of her Boston puppies eleven years ago and Cindy had a conversion. She said she loved her Dobermans, but Bostons were different from any dog she had known. "The dog is unique. They love you like no other animal. They sleep in your bed and follow you around the house. They dive under the blankets to be your foot warmer. Take this guy here," she said, indicating her puppy. "If I leave the room he cries." Fortunately, Cindy had not tattooed a Doberman on her leg and so was able to switch breed alliances.

I told her how drawn I was to Bostons, but that my family had pressured me to get a beagle. She shook her head. "That's a field dog," she said, looking at me with pity.

When Cindy's first Boston died, she said, "It was like an empty hole. I thought, I can't get another one, this hurt too bad." But three weeks later she announced to her husband she was ready for a new Boston. He said okay and she said, "I mean *now*." She opened the newspaper and found a Boston for sale.

She named that dog Mischief. "He was a Houdini. He got out of everything. I got an electric fence, a shock collar. I had him in a six-foot-high pen with a cover on it and he would escape." She said that one day she put him in the pen, made of chain-link fence, and a few minutes later saw him running past the house. She captured him and put him back, then looked through the window to see how he had made his getaway. "He climbed the chain link like he was a kid on a jungle gym. Then he shoved his head through a crack between the sides and the top." Unsurprisingly, Mischief's life was cut short when he was hit by a car.

By then there was no question that Cindy was getting another Boston. She contacted a breeder who was advertising a show-quality puppy. She took her son for the drive to the breeder's house, but when she got there hours later, the breeder said the show puppy had just been sold.

"I realize now that was a lie," said Cindy. It was a breeder trick—get you to the house with your heart set on going home with a dog, then sell you a leftover. The breeder said, "I do have an ugly one," and went to fetch her. The dog was as promised. Said Cindy, "She's the ugliest thing you've ever seen. She has a white face, and a big round head and extremely bulging eyes. Her white face makes her eyes look even more bulging." Her son fell in love with this freakish creature, so Cindy paid $100, took her home, and named her Diamond.

"She's the best pet I've ever had in my life. I would toss out my husband before my Diamond. She's been blind for three years."

Oh, no, I thought, I can't take any more.

"How did she go blind?" I asked.

"I had another Boston who was an aggressive bitch, which is very unusual. She had puppies and became dominant and started fighting with Diamond." I didn't have the heart to tell Cindy this was as unusual as a general who has just staged a military coup liquidating the members of the previous regime.

"The vet told me to stop the aggressive dog by shooting her with a squirt gun," Cindy continued. "It worked for three days. Then they passed each other and the younger dog bit Diamond and severed her optic nerve." I thought I would have to get on the floor and put my head between my legs to keep from passing out. Diamond has adjusted fine, she said, except for the time they had the house painted and all the furniture rearranged.

I had to leave and on my way out Sylvie, of Boston Terrier Rescue, introduced me to the head of the local Boston Terrier Fanciers Association. Sylvie explained I was interested in fostering a Boston. When the head of the association heard that, her eyes popped open so far that she resembled her favorite breed. By this time I was starting to reconsider my plan. Given that Sasha initiated dog play by biting her companion on the head, I was terrified that their first day together Sasha might end up swallowing the new dog's eyes. Or that I would pick up little Bosco and give it a squeeze and its eyes would pop out and roll across the kitchen floor.

I contemplated these horrors as I walked across the room, but every few feet I was stopped by a nudging at my knee. I looked down and there would be one of those crazy gremlin faces, tongue hanging out, eyes intact, looking up at me begging me to love it.

15

"THE DOG FOR US"

Gorgeous Annie, our latest foster.

It was probably for the best that my foster Boston plans were disrupted with a call from Laura. She had the perfect next beagle for us, Annie. Annie was a pet whose owner was dying of cancer and was forced to put Annie in a shelter. There are regulations at shelters about how long they have to hold a stray in order to give the owner a chance to come forward. But owner give-ups are in a much more precarious position and can end up quickly euthanized. But the shelter workers wanted to save Annie and so contacted BREW. Her BREW write-up said she had been a much-loved pet, probably too much loved given that she resembled a small dirigible. I agreed to take her.

When I picked her up at the vet's office where she was boarding, I was struck by her resemblance to Elizabeth Taylor during the period she was married to Senator John Warner, still gorgeous but needing to wear caftans. Annie's features were delicate and striking, most noticeable were her bright hazel eyes rimmed with dramatic black liner. She had a luscious, thick coat, as if she were draped in some sugar daddy's gift of mink. Despite her girth she had a beautiful woman's confidence in her desirability. She jumped in my lap with the full expectation she would be welcome, regardless of the damage to my spleen.

Annie's personality was less immediately apparent than either Roscoe's or Maggie's. Unlike Sasha, who still gave sidelong glances, Annie engaged with a stare that was, in parts, challenging, bold, and empty. She was the roughest of our foster dogs, responding to Sasha's head-biting play initiation with an I'm-not-kidding head-biting counterattack. The thick black fur on the back of her neck bristled, giving her the look of a boar that had had miraculous cosmetic surgery.

After a session with Sasha, she would return to her neutral posture. This absence of personality we realized was her personality, and had its own appeal, the way tofu's blandness becomes its selling point. I often took her to pick up my daughter at elementary school. The children streamed to her like magnetic filings, and she stoically took their abuse. One precocious kindergartner came over and said, "She's a dog like Snoopy. But Snoopy's ears are usually like this—" At that he took Annie's ears and held them straight up like exclamation points. A second-grade girl asked if she could walk Annie. After a few minutes she threaded the leash down her middle and out at her tail and said, "If you hold the leash like this, you can walk her backward!" I would always intervene before the children drove Annie completely nuts, but her threshold seemed particularly high.

She also was a great licker. At the end of the day, when I kicked my shoes off, she would be drawn to my sweaty feet and give them a thorough tongue bath. I had spent a lifetime futilely trying to get someone to suck on my toes. Now here was Annie who didn't even ask for a tit for toe in return.

It was easy to give her a glowing review on the BREW Web

site (although I left out my kinky sideline). Soon we had a phone
call from an interested childless, though not pregnant, couple. I
had a long conversation with the wife, who wanted to know how
Annie got along with other dogs because they had a twelve-year-
old beagle, Ernie, who was slowly dying. The dog had cancer,
kidney failure, heart problems—he was bloated to almost seventy
pounds because of steroids and his failing organs. They needed
a gentle new dog, the wife said, who would not harass their sickly
old one. I realized they were hoping their new dog would act as
grief insurance when their beloved Ernie finally died. If they
already had the new dog in place, then they would be less distraught at Ernie's end.

They came over and sat down on the couch and Annie immediately went to each of them, giving them a few licks and offering
her lovely head to pat. She rolled over for a belly rub. She went
with them for a walk and didn't pull on her leash. The visit took
about an hour and as they left I expected them to gush over her,
but instead they sounded noncommittal. "We're also interested
in Liesl, who looks like a nice dog. We're going to visit her," said
the wife. Liesl? Why would they visit another dog after this per-
formance by Annie—what more could they want?

I was offended, and when I looked at Liesl on the Web site I
thought her eyes were too close together. "Look at this," I said
to my husband. "They would compare her to Annie?" My husband was struck by their lack of enthusiasm, but identified the
problem. Instead of grief insurance, the reality of bringing home
a new dog had become a source of guilt. It was like a husband
clearing out space in his wife's closet, while she was breathing
her last in their bed, for the younger replacement he'd already
picked out.

Because they'd come and seen her, the couple had put Annie on
their reserve list, blocking other potential adopters. When more

than a week went by with no decision from them, Laura forwarded my phone number to a family that had seen Annie on the Web site.

The father called and explained he had two sons, ten and seven, and the youngest was mildly autistic. "I'm really interested in Annie," he said. "I think she has the right combination of qualities for our household." I too felt certain they had to have Annie. I could just see her making an emotional connection with the little boy, and being understanding of any quirks in his behavior.

They came over two nights later. The husband and older son sat on the couch and Annie jumped up and sprawled herself across their laps. She gave a few licks and presented her ample belly. Within minutes the husband was saying, "This is it. I knew she was the one." The son put his face in her coat and said, "I love you, Annie." The mother tried to guide the younger son, who was very articulate but jumpy, over to Annie. He seemed uncomfortable and she didn't push it.

"Laura also wants us to see Erin," the father said, mentioning another dog on the Web site. "I don't want to see Erin. This is the dog for us." Annie licked the older son's face and he laughed. The family knew that they were second in line for her, but I told them I would do what I could. That night I called Laura begging her to give Annie to them. She agreed the couple with the dying beagle had lost their place. I called the family that night and they said first thing in the morning they would go to the pet store for supplies then come by our house.

"Here's Annie! Here's Annie! Here's Annie! Here's Annie!" said the youngest son when they all came inside. They put the leash on her and we all walked to their van. They had a huge crate in the back and Annie hopped in and settled down. About a week later the wife sent me a photo by e-mail. It was of the youngest son and Annie. They were lying on the floor curled together like a quotation mark. The son was on the outside with his arms around Annie and a beatific look on his face. The mother wrote of the photo, "He's learned that dogs are good to love." My eyes welled up and my chin quivered.

I was now becoming one of those sappy, "dog love is better than any kind of love," "let's swap stories about our poochies" dog person. I was in danger of a descent into dog bathos. What if I ended up like my mother, wearing lockets filled with my foster dogs' hair?

16

BREWING UP TROUBLE

The strange dogs of the founder of BREW.

Since Laura Charles, the founder of BREW, was now more important to me than my hairdresser or internist, I had to find out more about how this intelligent, accomplished woman came to devote her life to beagles. We met for lunch in downtown D.C., where she worked at the Treasury Department. Laura is in her early thirties, speaks Russian, has a degree in international relations, is a wife and mother of two young children. She also puts between twenty to forty unpaid hours a week into BREW.

She traced back her obsession to a childhood dog, a rottweiler named Caesar. Caesar spent his life outdoors chained to his canine barracks; Laura's father was in the army and he believed spartan accommodations were strength building. Young Laura didn't think this was right, but as she was still in elementary school, she did not have the standing to countermand her father's orders. Poor Caesar was eventually buried, but never praised.

Laura grew up, studied in Russia, and returned with a Russian husband. At which point, she decided she needed a dog of her own. Somewhere along the line she developed the notion that happy families have golden retrievers, so she and her husband bought one from a breeder whose ad they saw in the newspaper. (Since I missed the happy-family-equals-golden-retriever myth, I did some research and realized Laura, who is fifteen years younger than I am, was probably moved as a girl by the sight of President Ford's family gathered around their golden retriever, Liberty, with her new puppies.)

They named the puppy Truman (confirming my notion that there was a presidential connection to her golden fixation). A few months later the breeder called and said a puppy was being returned because the owners were getting divorced. Did she and her husband want it? They did, and named it Jackson.

Jackson was not aware of his responsibility to contribute to his family's happiness. Actually, Jackson seemed to possess unhappy-family voodoo; not too long after his arrival, Laura's husband left her. Laura was not the kind of person who would return a dog because of a divorce. Instead, she started reading online personals looking for other dog lovers. She found one, they met and hit it off, and soon she and Russ and Truman and Jackson were living together in a town house. They weren't quite ready for marriage and children, but they were ready to get a dog of their own together.

As a boy, Russ had had a beagle named Banjo. Like Laura's rottweiler, Banjo had had an emotionally deprived yet long life chained in the backyard. They both realized they could redeem Banjo's memory by bringing joy to another beagle. "We didn't know enough," said Laura. "We knew beagles couldn't be taken off-leash, but we didn't know how hard they were to house-train." Not knowing enough beforehand is the key to all major life decisions. Who would ever get married, have children, buy a house, let alone get a dog, if you knew enough?

Laura and Russ found a couple who had mated their beagle with some passing dog so their children could see the miracle of birth. That accomplished, they now wanted the miracles out of the house. When Laura and Russ arrived one of the puppies was adorably chewing on another puppy's head. They couldn't bear to separate the two playmates, so they bought both the chewer, whom they named Petey, and the chewed, who became Flip.

It was not long after they brought the beagles home that they realized what they thought was playfulness was actually canni-balism. That misinterpretation has subjected Flip to what Laura calls a life of "eternal damnation." It turned out Petey, who had bad teeth, an overactive thyroid, and separation anxiety, was an aggressive alpha dog. Laura and Russ returned home from work each day to find their walls splattered with blood, the result of Petey's attempts to eat Flip's ears and lips. Petey was so aggres-sive that he started biting Truman. In a few weeks the fourteen-pound puppy had the seventy-five-pound golden retriever curled up in the fetal position. Neither of the beagles was housebroken, of course, nor in a mood to be. Also, the first night they got the dogs, they let Petey sleep in the bed with them. "He now weighs forty-five pounds. He sleeps on Russ's side," said Laura.

Not every moment was unrelieved horror. There was the time the beagles discovered a pair of panty hose in the laundry basket and realized it was the perfect vehicle for tug-of-war. Each dog took hold of a foot, and started pulling as they piled out of the dog door and into the yard. There they managed to stretch the panty hose to about twenty feet. In the middle of the yard was a single tree which Petey and Flip started running around like a maypole. As each dog chased the other, the panty hose started wrapping around the tree, eventually binding both Petey and Flip, who were now fixed against the trunk. The solution to their predicament was obvious: let go of the foot. But Petey was not going to because he was the alpha dog, and Flip was not going to because for once he had found a way to keep Petey away from his lips and ears. There they were bound, growling, until, as if by mutual agreement, each opened his mouth, the panty hose foot fell out, and they tumbled off the tree.

But the constant growling, baying, barking, and cries of pain emitted from the town house during the day caused Laura and Russ's neighbors to report them to animal control, so they had to move. By this time Laura and Russ were married. In retrospect their daily misery showed them how strong their bond was. "This stuff with the dogs would have jeopardized a weaker new marriage," Laura said.

Laura's father suggested they get rid of the dogs as a wedding present to themselves. Something about what he said made sense—the young couple could come home each night to a house not covered in blood and feces. But Laura couldn't do it. She had a beaglelike stubbornness. She found a townhouse that would accept all four dogs, and also discovered an online chat room for people with beagles and beagle trouble. The online community encouraged her to stick with it, and through them, Laura found out about the world of rescue dogs.

Laura began volunteering for the local golden retriever rescue group. She started by helping at adoption days. This escalated to taking in foster goldens, which did not add to the serenity of their home. One, a malnourished golden, discovered a dog biscuit had been kicked under the couch. She was too big, however, to crawl under the sofa to get it. So like some oil wildcatter determined to find a deposit, she drilled down through the couch, removing the upholstery until she exposed the wood frame, and got the biscuit.

"I would be up at two A.M., crying because a dog had just eaten my sofa, with stitches in my hand from Petey, and I would just keep going," she said.

"Stitches in your hand?" I said, shocked. She just nodded with a delphic smile. The Laura in front of me seemed happy and well adjusted. But I couldn't help but think of the story I'd read of a criminal defense attorney who had fallen in love with one of her sociopath clients and ran off with him.

Laura switched from golden rescue to an organization that took in all breeds. Besides working full-time, she added an almost full-time load of volunteer work. She picked up dogs from shelters, took them to foster homes, and did home-checks on potential adopters. There were so many unwanted beagles that she made a special effort to place them.

One situation was typical, animal control had been called to a farm with seventeen sick, starved beagles. Only one tiny one, the breeding female, could be saved. Laura named the dog Noelle and took her in temporarily, a situation that has lasted four years. Noelle is pathologically shy, blind in one eye, has a swollen liver, and a heart murmur. She is a ghostly presence in the house. "Only a few people have ever seen her," said Laura, making Noelle sound like the mad wife confined to the attic in *Jane Eyre*. Because Noelle hasn't attacked anyone, and is housebroken, Laura calls her "the nice one."

Laura's soft spot for beagles eventually brought her into conflict with the head of the all-breed organization who warned her to stop with the beagles because Laura was giving the group a reputation for being "too hound heavy."

In February of 1999, Laura, pregnant with her first child, and Russ were driving two abandoned beagle puppies to a foster home when Laura was struck with an idea. Why not start her own beagle rescue organization? Russ, instead of saying, "Honey, you're pregnant. The hormones are making you deranged," said, "You could call it Beagle Rescue Education and Welfare." They named themselves the board of directors, vowed that if they ever spent more than $150 of their own money they'd stop doing it, and decided that the puppies in the back were their first place-ment. "There was a bull terrier rescue and they are placing about thirty-five dogs a year," she said. "There was a komondor rescue and there are twelve komondors in the whole country." Laura realized there were endless abandoned beagles and no one to speak up for them.

But after her experience with Petey and Flip, how could she inflict beagles on naïve people deluded by years of Charles Schulz cartoons? Laura, ever honest, knew she couldn't push the Snoopian image of a dog that wrestled with philosophical quan-daries from atop its doghouse. She made sure people knew these salient beagle qualities: stubborn, loud, will eat until they explode, difficult to train, impossible to let run loose. Yes, they sound like men. And like men, they can be good to cuddle with, loyal, and have irresistible, soulful eyes.

In the years since she founded BREW Laura has placed more than two thousand beagles. She tries not to dwell on the fact that almost every dog she has placed has turned out to be a good pet. "I'm not bitter but I am perturbed that I have two pain-in-the-ass beagles. They are badly bred, have multiple health problems, need to be medicated every day, and they don't even like my kids. Oh, if it's raining, Petey won't go outside, so he pees and poops in the laundry room." Petey, demonstrating a wily survival instinct, has never attacked the children, ages four and two—he bites the kids and he's a goner, says Laura. Instead he runs and hides from them. Because Noelle is already hiding, she has little contact with the children. Flip is uninterested.

I asked Laura what she does with her dogs when she goes away.

"We don't go away," she said. "The last time we did, I had to put the dogs in five different places—all to various BREW volun-teers. Unfortunately Petey pooped on the floor and destroyed the blinds. So he had to get sent to an animal hospital to be boarded. While he was there he bit the vet tech."

"How old is Petey?" I asked.

"Not old enough. He and Flip are only five." With the founding of BREW, her ability to make any kind of "other arrangements" for Petey ended. "I can't put him down. Every vet in the Mid-Atlantic knows me. I'm not going to let him go and get hit by a car. I can't give him up to BREW because our rule is that if you give up a dog, you can't get another. What are my options?" It was the most satisfying lunch I'd ever had.

17

BEWARE OF DOG

Not every dog is as good as Sasha.

Talking to Laura made me appreciate what a sweet, gentle dog I had. I'd never had a moment's concern about Sasha attacking anyone, especially me. Yet, I still had a longing for a Boston terrier, despite the loose-eyeball issue. Walking back home from the drugstore one day, I saw walking quickly ahead of me a young man and a medium-sized dog with erect ears and the telltale black-and-white coat. It had to be a Boston—on my street! I hurried to catch up with the owner to talk about Bostons. The man was a speed walker and I was panting when I reached him. "Hi, is that a Boston terrier?" I asked, as I looked at the dog's sturdy body and squashed-in face.

"I think he's a mix," said the man.

"Are you the owner?" I asked.

"No, I'm the dog walker."

"He really looks like a Boston terrier, he has—" I was about to say that the dog, who had been looking at me intently, had a classic Boston face, when I was interrupted by his leaping the foot-and-a-half distance that separated us to greet me.

This is what my brain said—that this Boston terrier, like the dozens of others at the dog show, was coming over to nuzzle my leg and get me to pat him. My brain kept saying this as I noticed he was not exactly nuzzling me, more hanging from me, hanging from my left thigh where he had clamped his jaws and was now vibrating them like a pair of trick dentures. I was still trying to process this unusual greeting when I felt a fast-traveling message moving through my body, like an e-mail zipping through cyberspace. When this message got to my brain I saw that the subject line was "JAWS!" I was being attacked.

The dog walker too was so unnerved by his charge that he simply stood there, holding the leash, now taut from the exertions of the hanging dog. The dog walker and I looked at each other, and finally the dog walker snapped the leash back and screamed, "Alastair!" causing the creature to come tumbling off my leg.

"He bit me," I said, thinking, What is this dog a mix of, Boston terrier and velociraptor?

"Wow. Sorry. He's never done that before," the walker said. He was pale and shaking, in worse shape than I was. I realized I was contemplating a swollen leg and he was contemplating the end of his job.

Before I left I knew I had to at least find out who the owners were to check if Alastair was current on his shots. I suddenly saw myself as a brief, comic item on the Drudge Report: WOULD-BE DOG BOOK WRITER KILLED BY RABID DOG.

The walker read the address and phone number off Alastair's tag, I jotted it down and limped home. I stripped off my saliva-drenched jeans and saw that I had a softball-sized lump emerging from my thigh. There were abrasions but no teeth marks. Levi Strauss was responsible for my possessing an intact thigh. If I had been wearing a skirt I could have become the author of *The Alastair System for Instant Thigh Reduction.* I showered, put an ice pack on my leg, and called my doctor, who was also a friend. He quickly called back.

"I don't mean to laugh," he said, laughing. "But you've got to admit your getting bitten by a dog is pretty ironic." I told him I'd already made that observation.

"You need to come down for a tetanus shot and I'm going to put you on antibiotics," he said. I told him the dog hadn't punctured the skin. He asked me to describe my leg and when I mentioned "softball" he said, "That's a deep injury. You don't want to get an infection there."

It was time for me to pick my daughter up. I put on a long skirt and, making sure Alastair wasn't lurking about, walked the five minutes to her school. When I got there, I told her I had been bitten by a dog and lifted my skirt to show her. The softball was turning purple—my leg looked like Krakatoa about to erupt.

"What happened, Mom!" she said, horrified. I told her about seeing the Boston terrier and how it attacked me for no reason.

She replied with the tone Ward Cleaver reserved for talks in his study after one of Beaver's particularly boneheaded adventures. "Mom, I am not surprised. Mom, look at a Boston terrier. Their eyes are sticking out. When a dog is going to bite you, its eyes start to stick out. That's why I told you we could not have a Boston terrier. You see what I'm talking about, Mom?"

Early that evening I called Alastair's owners. They weren't home but their answering-machine greeting was "Karen, Bill, and Alastair aren't here. Please leave a message." I thought this was good news and bad news. The good news was that people who put their dog on their answering machine were likely to have a dog that was up-to-date on his rabies shots. The bad news was that such people were also likely to say I must have provoked their sweet baby into attacking. I left a message.

They called me back a few hours later, both of them on the line. They were abjectly apologetic, but not totally surprised.

"I'm so, so sorry. He's on Prozac, but I guess it's not working," Karen said, choking up. I thought, Prozac? How about one of those darts they use on *National Geographic* specials that drop rampaging elephants.

"Has he bitten anyone else?" I asked.

Bill replied, "No, but we've had incidents before. He's barked and lunged in an aggressive manner. We've been working with a behaviorist who says he's afraid and is mixing up fight or flight." *He's* afraid? It sounded like the kind of excuse made for playground bullies: Oh, the poor thing is expressing his insecurity.

I said that they needed to have the dog muzzled when he went out in public. Karen responded tearfully, "He has such a small, flat face that no muzzle will fit!"

Bill apologized for the fiftieth time and said they would of course pay any medical expenses.

I am a person who has gone swimming in gym shorts just to avoid having to wear a bathing suit, but the next day I put on a skirt and lifted it to virtually anyone I knew to show this livid lump, now as big as a grapefruit. It was as if this was some great accomplishment. I also enjoyed the repulsed reactions (which may have been partly due to the fact that I hadn't yet gone for a seasonal leg-waxing). I got my tetanus shot and my doctor gratifyingly said, upon seeing the wound, "Now that's impressive."

By then I had looked up "dog bite" on the Centers for Disease Control Web site. According to the government, I should have been hearing a lot of dog-bite stories. The CDC estimates there are about 4.7 million dog-bite incidents yearly in the United States.

About 800,000 people require medical care, and 334,000 end up in the emergency room. That's bad, but given that there are about 68 million pet dogs in the United States, death by dog bite is extremely rare: an average of fewer than twenty cases a year. Compare that with the approximately eighty-two yearly deaths due to lightning strikes. I discovered, however, it's much safer to be in the middle of a field being chased by a mad dog with a thunderstorm coming in, than it is to take a bath. Each day in America someone dies in the bathtub.

I kept the news about bubble baths to myself when Alastair's father came over to give me a check to pay for my medical expenses. Of course, I showed him the bite and he closed his eyes and swayed a little. I said, "You've got a real problem. Your dog is small and cute and a kid could run up to pet him and—" I waved my finger across my throat. Several people had advised me to report the bite to the police. I did consider it—as a public-safety issue—but I felt the owners were sufficiently aware of Alastair's dangers.

Bill sat down to write the check and Sasha ran over, jumped on the couch, sat next to him, and placed her head on his lap. He patted her and she gave him an adorable look with her big, brown eyes. There was no need for me to actually say, "Now that's how a dog is supposed to behave."

I asked Bill if Alastair was a mix.

"No, he's pure Boston terrier." Just as I'd thought. He said they'd gotten Alastair as a puppy four years ago. For the first three years of his life he was a typical, happy Boston terrier. Then he went psycho. None of the many veterinarians they'd consulted had been any help, so they were exchanging e-mails with a renowned animal behaviorist in Boston. (I wondered if there was some kind of law at work here. If you have a crazy Dutch Smoushond your behaviorist has to live in Amsterdam, for a loony Pekingese you look for a therapist in Beijing.)

The behaviorist's theory was that several recent moves the family had made fritzed out the territorial part of Alaistair's brain and that he felt he had to defend his property. Bill said that they put him on such a high dose of Prozac that he became lethargic and unresponsive. (Good!) So they lowered it and now it wasn't working at all. They were also in touch with a trainer who had been recommended to them but they hadn't been able to arrange an appointment yet.

"We know we have to keep him away from people. Maybe we can only let him out in the backyard and he can't even be walked," Bill said. I imagined Alastair becoming like Norma Desmond in *Sunset Boulevard*: trapped in the house, obsessing about the glorious past, and becoming more deranged and homicidal.

A few weeks later I took Sasha for a group class with Todd. I said to him, "I've got to tell you about being attacked by a dog." He narrowed his eyes and said, "What breed?"

"Boston terrier."

"*You're* the lady Alastair attacked!" he said. It turned out Todd was the dog trainer Bill and Karen had been trying to enlist.

"That is the meanest dog I have ever encountered in my life," said Todd. He described going to their house and Bill coming to the door to shake Todd's hand, while holding the snarling Alastair on the leash in his other hand.

"I said, 'Step back, I don't want to shake your hand that bad.' That dog was snapping like he wanted to get a piece of me. I said to them, 'If that dog touches me I am kicking it.'" I thought Todd's approach might be more effective than a long psychological tour of Alastair's past to see whether his mother was a bitch.

Todd said he had gotten a bark collar on Alastair, which gave him a shock every time he acted aggressive. It seemed to be having

some effect. Then Todd shook his head. "Mean dog. *Mean dog.*
I told those people you better hope the lady he bit is a dog lover.
And you are!"

Perhaps the whole incident was a sign: Stick with beagles.

18

THERE ARE NO BAD DOGS

Well, maybe a few naughty ones.

When I told my brother about my encounter with Alastair, he told me about his own adventure with a disturbed dog. As a boy, my brother was a prolific trash scavenger, with a gift for finding treasures among our neighbors' garbage. My grandmother was always horrified. "It's covered with germs," she said at whatever he brought in. "Touch it and it will go right to your brain!" One day, after he was newly married, his childhood instinct was aroused by the sight of a stray dog wandering near the Dumpster at his apartment building in Cambridge, Massachusetts.

This dog, let's call him "Dumpster," was the kind of wily, urban dog that exists in a realm outside breeds. Breeds are for sissies. The dog looked like he had a gray coat, but it was impossible to determine if the gray was due to age or matted dirt. A chunk of his ear was missing and the rough patches on his body were either scars from encounters with crazed raccoons or mange. His eyes gleamed and his teeth didn't. "I thought he might make a good pet," my brother said.

The dog was curious about Doug but wary. Doug went into his apartment and got a can of corned beef hash. He put a little in a bowl and placed it at the rear door to the building. The dog got close to the food and Doug, then ran away before eating it. Doug spoke soothingly, and the dog came closer, lifting the left corner of his upper lip which gave him a striking resemblance to Sylvester Stallone. The food disappeared faster than the human retina was able to register. Holding out the bowl, Doug lured Dumpster into the building. He put the dog in his apartment and went out and got cans of dog food, a collar, and leash. When Doug's wife, Patty, came home the dog was sleeping in the living room.

Patty was appalled. She was finishing her training as a doctor, and while she didn't subscribe to Doug's grandmother's theory about trash germs going to your brain, she thought that when Dumpster awoke he might have the capacity to rip out their brains. But she had never seen such a look of paternal caring on Doug's face before, so she agreed to give Dumpster a chance.

That evening when Doug put the collar and leash on Dumpster to take him out, Dumpster acted as if Doug was trussing him up to walk him down death row. But when they got outside Dumpster did his business quickly and eagerly returned to the apartment, apparently realizing freedom's just another word for no corned beef hash. When it was time for them to go to bed, Doug left Dumpster in the living room and he and Patty shut the bedroom door. "Within minutes he was throwing himself against the bedroom door, and howling," said Doug. Dumpster loved them already!

They could never sleep through the thudding and howling, so they decided to let Dumpster into the room. He immediately jumped into bed between them. What a wonderful dog! They stroked Dumpster, then turned to go to sleep. Their movements tripped something in Dumpster. Suddenly he was up on all fours, tense and alert. He emitted a low growl and surveyed the couple.

Doug and Patty, looking at their blanket-wrapped bodies from Dumpster's perspective, realized they resembled a pair of enormous, quivering maggots. "I started to lift my hand from under the covers so I could pat him and calm him down," recalled Doug. "He pounced and grabbed my hand in his jaws, and started growling." The pressure from the dog's teeth on his blanket-covered arm was not enough to pierce the skin, but it was enough to make Doug not want to see how much more pressure that would take. He involuntarily called out and Patty, who had tried to settle down to sleep, turned to see what was the matter. At that, Dumpster let go of Doug and jumped to Patty, placing his teeth on her left shoulder.

"Don't move and he won't bite," Doug told his wife.

Doug understood that all Dumpster needed to become a good pet was love, a decent meal, a shot of Thorazine, and a stun gun.

While Dumpster held on to Patty's shoulder, Doug gingerly sat up. At this Dumpster released Patty and Doug grabbed the dog by the collar and put him in the bathroom. He got back into bed, but within minutes Dumpster was howling and hurling himself against the door. After another few minutes, the upstairs neighbors began rhythmically pounding on Doug and Patty's ceiling, conveying in apartment dweller's Morse code, "Shut up down there." Exercising the kind of judgment that allows people to say, "We don't need a field guide. I can tell which mushrooms are edible," Doug let Dumpster out of the bathroom. He jumped back on the bed.

The couple pretended to be asleep, the kind of sleep in which you lie flat on your back, staring at the ceiling, your limbs arranged with the angular precision of a Pinocchio doll. Dumpster, sensing his new owners had turned to wood, settled down between them in a ragged slumber. While he dreamt, he growled at imaginary euthanasia squads, or fellow strays who hoarded boxes of fried chicken. When Doug or Patty drifted off, causing some part of their body to jerk involuntarily, Dumpster jumped to his feet, his jaws fastened to the offending limb. "You could call it a long night," said Doug.

Morning came and the three of them got out of bed early. Doug put half a can of food into Dumpster's bowl, and Patty set out cereal and milk on the dining room table. As soon as the milk hit the corn flakes Dumpster ran to the table. Then, in a move that should be studied by all participants in standing high jump competitions, Dumpster managed to go from having four paws on the floor to having four paws on the dining room table. His front feet in the cereal bowls, Dumpster began licking at the milk spilling out of the overturned carton.

"Doug, get this dog out of here now!" Patty screamed.

Doug put Dumpster on his leash and took him to the car. Doug was working at a construction site and they drove there together. He didn't know what to do. He remembered some old saying or legend or curse that once you've saved someone's life you're obligated to help that person forever. Did it come from the Bible or a fortune cookie? Did it apply to dogs as well as people? And why should you be obligated to the person you saved—shouldn't it be the other way around?

Still, Doug couldn't shake the feeling that he had some further responsibility to this creature, that he couldn't just throw Dumpster back to the world that tortured him even in his sleep. He got to the construction site and let the dog out of the car and took off his leash. Dumpster kept Doug within close range. After about a half hour on the job Doug noticed that Dumpster had gotten hold of what looked like a piece of pink rubber tubing and was crazily chewing on it. Doug sighed; he couldn't let the dog eat a piece of rubber.

He went over to Dumpster to see what was in his mouth. The

thing was pinkish and gnarled and about a foot long. Doug grabbed the long, thin, stiff end of it—was it a piece of wire?— and started pulling. The dog went mad and pulled all the harder on the fatter end. They pulled and pulled until finally Doug won with a yank. He looked at the misshapen thing hanging from his hand and realized it had a head. The head had a very clear expression on its face. The expression said, "Bubonic plague, anyone?" Doug was holding a mummified rat.

He threw it down and went inside the site's trailer. "I scrubbed my hands in the bathroom, then came out and found a phone book," said Doug. When the person on the other end said, "Humane Society," Doug said, "Hi, I think I've found a stray dog."

Sometimes a dog gets in trouble just for doing what it has been bred to do. Its gene pool bubbles up like an overheated hot tub. Marilyn, who lives near the ocean in Manhattan Beach, California, is the mother of four young children. Her oldest daughter had wanted a dog forever, and when the youngest child started kindergarten, Marilyn agreed they could get one. Marilyn and her daughter looked through dog books, and finally decided on a Portuguese water dog. Marilyn talked to the Portuguese water dog rescue people who said the number of young children in the family would upset a dog. Marilyn thought if she could deal with it, a dog should be able to deal with it, but the rescue people were adamant.

So back to the books they went, where they saw a new crossbreed, the labradoodle, half Labrador retriever, half poodle. "They are used for blind and handicapped people," said Marilyn, which meant they were patient and had a good temperament. "They don't shed, they don't smell. They were perfect."

The next day, while she was waiting to pick up her son at school, a woman walked by with an adorable dog with a curly coat. "I called out, What's that?" said Marilyn.

"It's a labradoodle," the woman answered. Marilyn thought, No way! She hadn't even heard of this dog until yesterday. It was obviously a sign.

"Where do you get one?" Marilyn asked.

"Australia," the woman answered.

Again Marilyn thought, No way! The woman said she didn't think that American labradoodles were being properly bred. The breed was started in Australia, and the finest labradoodle breeders were there, she insisted. Marilyn got the e-mail address for the woman's breeder and started corresponding. She explained to the breeder that because of her four children she wanted a dog past puppy stage. The breeder had just the thing, a beautiful year-old silver dog.

By this time, the passing stranger with the labradoodle had become Marilyn's labradoodle consultant. She gave advice on how to get your dog from Australia to Los Angeles, and where to find the best vet, trainer, and groomer.

The dog, which the family decided to name Nickel, cost $3,400. Flying Nickel on Qantas Airways cost an additional $5,000. Marilyn thought that for $8,400 this better be quite a dog. He was. "I have four kids and my husband travels a lot, and my dog is awesome." He was playful, easygoing, and responsible. "When my youngest one goes to sleep, Nickel will stay in the room with him for a little while just to check on him." The family drove from Los Angeles to Iowa for vacation—four kids and a dog in a truck—and Nickel wasn't a minute of trouble. "I love him," Marilyn told me.

Several months after they got Nickel, Marilyn's five-year-old had a playdate with a boy from school Marilyn had not met before. The family lived next to the beach and when it was time to get her son Marilyn and Nickel walked to pick him up. The mother was a gracious woman from Argentina who invited

Marilyn in so they could get acquainted. The woman was a dentist whose passionate hobby was surfing. The whole family—she had a kindergartner and a first-grader—had just returned from a surfing vacation in Fiji, the woman said. As Marilyn walked in, she noticed they had a bird and a rabbit that were out of their cages so the children could play with them.

In the front hallway, the floor was covered with sandy flip-flops. "Nickel is not a terrible chewer, but all those flip-flops looked enticing and I was worried he would start chewing them. I said to my son, 'Hold Nickel while I peek into the house.' And I went in."

The mother was showing Marilyn around when from the next room she heard her son scream, "Nickel, NO!"

Both mothers ran in to see Nickel proudly holding the family's parrot in his mouth. Marilyn screamed, "Nickel, drop it!" and out of his mouth fell a gorgeous blue tropical bird. Besides being nonshedding, nonallergenic, patient, and good with kids, a labradoodle is a cross between two breeds of dogs whose original purpose was to accompany hunters to retrieve birds.

Bird dogs were bred not to crush or eat the birds, but hold them in their mouths and return them whole to the hunter. The parrot that fell out of Nickel's mouth was intact, except for a few poke holes from which blood was trickling. By this time all the children were screaming and crying. The mother very calmly picked up the bird and put her thumb over its heart—she had medical training, after all.

"Children, the heart is slowing down," she said in her melodious accent. "It is very slow now, children. Our bird is dying . . . Children, our bird is dead."

Marilyn was standing there, holding Nickel, dumbstruck.

"Come here, children," the mother said, beckoning them closer. "In the jungle, this is what happens. This is the cycle of life. We will bury him. He had a good life."

Marilyn's brain was racing. Had her $8,400 dog just killed some $9,000 bird from Fiji? What could she say? Do I immediately offer to buy a new one, or does that sound too cold? she thought.

Her thoughts were interrupted by her son saying, "At least it wasn't the bunny."

Then her son's playmate said, "You have to buy us a new bird!" Marilyn recalled thinking, "Of course it now looks like a six-year-old comes up with the right thing to do and I couldn't."

The mother said to Marilyn, "We'll talk about this later."

Marilyn, apologizing profusely, left with her son and dog. By the time she got home there was a message from the woman: "Please don't be upset. I know it was an accident."

Marilyn volunteers at the school library twice a month and the first time she went there after the incident her son's playmate refused to look at her. Two weeks later, when he handed her his book he said, "Your dog killed my bird." The next time he said, "You feel really bad your dog killed my bird." The time after that he said, "When are you going to buy us a bird?" The following time he hugged Marilyn.

Since then the boy has become a regular visitor to Marilyn's house. "He loves Nickel," she said. "He doesn't hold him responsible." Eventually, the mother called and said the family was ready for a new bird, and that if Marilyn still wanted to, she could buy it. Marilyn was relieved to hear they weren't looking for anything exotic. Something about one percent of what she paid for Nickle would do just fine.

19

INCONTINENCE CAN BE FUN

"I think you should smell something in the basement."

If you were a client of Todd's, you could board your dog with him. The day before we left for two weeks in New England, Todd came by to pick up Sasha. She now greeted him not only with equanimity, but immediately sat, as if all she ever did was anticipate a master's command. I thought this revealed an Eddie Haskell–like side of her personality. I watched through the window as Todd walked her to his van. She trotted along happily until she seemed to recognize that in crossing the street with Todd ownership had passed to him. They got to the opposite sidewalk where his van was parked and Sasha sat down and refused to move. Todd gave her a little jerk on the leash; still she sat. I could read her mind: "Don't mind me, Todd, I'm not a dog, I'm just a toadstool here in the grass." He could read it too and picked her up and put her next to him in the front seat.

Knowing that Sasha was with Todd allowed us to go on vacation without worry. Maybe, we even hoped, her two weeks there would play out like one of those movies about a reform school that turns a delinquent into a valedictorian. The first few days of our trip we wondered how she was doing. We decided she probably had this question for Todd: "Those other people—I never did learn their names—am I ever going to see them again?"

When we got back from vacation, Todd had already returned Sasha, who was waiting for us in the backyard. It was wonderful to see her; she had not turned into the valedictorian.

Our babysitter had house-sat for us, taking care of the cats while we were gone. She said everything had gone great. Then she added, almost as an afterthought, "I think you should smell something in the basement."

Instead of going to smell something in the basement, I thought we should keep our bags packed, call a cab, get dropped off at the railroad station, and start over as hobos. The life of a hobo could not smell as bad as what I knew awaited me in the basement.

I went to the basement. Our babysitter did not need to point out where the smell emanated from. My husband, daughter, and I all gingerly walked to a corner of the room. Had the cats uncovered a World War I mustard gas munitions dump? I touched the carpet; it was soaked. The cats were taking the popular injunction to "think outside the box" far too literally. I understood they might have been angry that we went on vacation, but weren't they thrilled that Sasha left, too?

It was obviously a form of civil disobedience inspired by the dogs. But it seemed a malevolent progression, sort of like SDS evolving into the Weathermen. I scrubbed, sprayed, powdered, and vacuumed the carpet to little effect. I assumed once we were back and everything settled down, the cats would return to normal. Instead the situation escalated. In the morning we found the bathmats as well as the rug by the sink in the kitchen wet with pee. We knew this time it wasn't Sasha, because she had been in her crate all night.

I embarked on an intense love-therapy program. I lay on the bed with the cats and rubbed and stroked them as they arched their backs and purred. My husband, observing one of these scenes, mentioned that he might like to get some of this action. I told him, "Start peeing on the bathmat, then get in line."

The loving had no effect—just the opposite, as the cats added new areas of the house to the list of litter-box substitutes. It was time to see the vet. I assumed the problem was psychological, but as soon as I started to describe the situation, I realized it was like discussing the emotional implications of irritable bowel syndrome with the plumber. The vet was just interested in whether the pipes were working right, at a cost of $250. "What if the cats are fine?" I asked, adding that every time I had paid for an expensive test, my animals were always fine.

"Then you've got a real problem," she said. "You should know there is only a fifty percent success rate in treating cat soiling."

"What happens if you're in the unlucky fifty?" I said, certain that was my destiny.

She shrugged then said, "You can keep the cats outside. You can get rid of them. Sometimes people move."

If we moved, were we supposed to sneak out in the middle of the night and not give the cats our forwarding address? Then she handed me a piece of paper. The vet was so busy and stressed she hadn't had time to reformat the advice sheet so it read, "Quick behavior tips (for the busy, stressed vet in a 15 minute appt)." The tips were for a litter box care program that was only slightly less consuming than embarking on a career as a concert pianist.

I was to get all new litter boxes, three for two cats. They needed to be scooped daily, then completely emptied and washed with scalding water weekly. When I got home I noticed that the instructions on the box of litter itself recommended replacing the litter only monthly. Even the cat litter company didn't have the nerve to try to quadruple their sales with a "dump weekly" program. Finding this schedule rather onerous, I went to the Internet for more advice. There was plenty. I should put litter boxes in each place where the cats soiled, to try to retrain them to use the box. This would mean stepping into a litter box upon getting out of a shower, and wearing a couple of litter boxes, like a pair of mukluks, as I stomped around the kitchen preparing dinner.

One site told me that cats are so sensitive to odors that if they smell even one molecule of their own urine in the box, they consider it beneath their dignity to use it. Hey, boys, I only clean my toilet once a week. Of course, another site told me when I cleaned the box I should return a small amount of soiled litter to it—if the cats *couldn't* smell their own pee, they wouldn't use the box. I read that I needed a litter box on every floor because the cats might resent having to take the stairs in order to relieve themselves. Well, *I* had to take the stairs in order to relieve myself. I was starting to feel they didn't need me, they needed a concierge.

A book I consulted had a chapter on reasons for soiling. Cats hate change, it noted, and such things as reupholstering a couch, or a family member getting a job with new work hours, could cause a cat to soil in protest. How was it that I'd had cats for twenty years and didn't realize that my obligation as a cat owner was to have myself, and all my belongings, frozen in amber? All the advice came with the warning that once a cat starts going out of the box, it can be impossible to solve. I felt as if I'd fallen into a fractured feline version of "The Princess and the Pee."

I called a carpet cleaning company and said I needed their Chernobyl-strength deodorizers. The woman on the other end laughed when I explained the problem was cats. "We can't guarantee that we can get all the cat odor out. No one can. It can't be done. We had one customer with a cat who peed so much on a basement carpet that he not only had to have the carpet replaced, he had to jackhammer out the concrete floor." I had to wait for her to compose herself so I could make an appointment.

I trudged into the little pet store nearby for my new supplies. When I told the owner I needed as many boxes of unscented litter as he had, he asked what was going on. His face lit with the glow a retailer gets when he knows he has a desperate sucker standing in his store. "I have the solution to your problem," he said, plucking a box off the shelf. It was a bottle of cat pheromone. You plugged it into an electrical socket, which heated the pheromone, wafting its scent all over the house. Both the proprietor and the manufacturer were a little shaky on how this olfactory stimulation communicated the message "Pee in the litter box." But what would the effect be on the rest of us? I had an image of my husband, daughter, and myself under the spell of the pheromone, spending the night alternately scratching the couch, and licking our private parts. The owner assured me the only effect it had on humans was to cause a $40 charge on the credit card for each bottle purchased. He suggested one for each floor.

After plugging in the pheromone and establishing a shrine to hygenic cat elimination in the basement, my husband and I took Sasha for a walk. We ran into a pair of cat-loving, dog-hating neighbors who thought we had been crazy to get a dog.

"How's it going?" Diane said, indicating Sasha.

"She's doing great," said my husband. "It's the cats who are driving us crazy now." We explained that just as Sasha had become housebroken, the cats had decided it was too much of an imposition. They nodded their heads with more than passing sympathy.

"The same thing happened to us," said Diane. She worked for the State Department and she and her husband, Marc, had lived all over the world, dragging along their cat, Attila. But unlike his namesake, who gloried in his bloody conquest of Europe, all the travel gave Attila the cat a breakdown. By the time they set up house in Turkey, Attila was peeing all over the baseboards of the rented apartment.

"Cat urine does devastating things to oak," Marc remembered.

They tried various litter box solutions, but nothing worked. They knew they would never get their security deposit back, and feared they would be kicked out of the apartment.

"Finally we had to give the cat to a friend who lived on a farm in the country," said Diane.

"See!" said my husband, turning to me. Giving the cats to a friend in the country had become his endlessly repeated solution.

"Unlike us, they had a friend who lived in the country!" I said.

It wasn't just the country, it was a fabulous spread in the Loire Valley. Their friend was a painter who did massive canvases that sold for between $10,000 and $50,000 each. One day he noticed an odd yellow stain in a corner of one painting. He looked at several other works; they all had the same weird stain right over his signature. He couldn't imagine what was going on until he walked in one day to find Attila lifting his leg and leaving his signature over the artist's own signature.

"What happened?" I asked.

It turned out that a friend who lives in the country is the last stop for an incorrigible pet.

"He had the cat put down," said Diane. "He said, 'Attila could have peed anywhere in the Loire Valley except on the paintings.'"

This was a sobering story. Sasha sat still through the telling, as if grasping its essential message.

The next day I got a call from the vet. Nothing was physically wrong with either cat. She suggested that it was possible only one was doing it and that I keep a closer eye on them. That evening I was in the basement doing laundry when Biscuit came down and, as if it was the most natural thing in the world, sat in the litter box to pee. Shortly afterward, I was walking by the upstairs bathroom when I saw Goldie, as if it was the most natural thing in the world, squat on the bathmat and pee.

This made me confront an essential difference between cats and dogs. Dogs are like beauty pageant entrants; they want to please. Once Sasha figured out going in the house was making us mad, she stopped. Cats are like supermodels; they want you to please them. Amazingly, our new program of litter box sterilization and wafting pheromones must have started pleasing Goldie. Over the next week there was a dramatic, if not complete, reduction in wet spots.

My husband was not mollified. My sister had a cat that was dying and my husband thought we should start making noises about the sacrifice we would be willing to make to ease her grief when the time came. "Tell her she shouldn't go too long without a new cat. And we have the perfect one for her."

20

ANIMAL
MISCOMMUNICATOR

I become a pet psychic.

Shortly after things started breaking down with the cats, I saw a small, intriguing advertisement in the weekly pet page section of the *Washington Post*. It was for a workshop in communicating telepathically with your pet. I thought being able to have telepathic conversations with the animals about bladder control might diminish the amount of urine I found around the house. And since I work at home, developing this skill would also reduce the time I spent talking to myself.

I looked up the Web site listed in the ad. It was for someone I'll call Delphine Carnack, professional animal communicator. Her Web site explained that we experience a constant two-way telepathic conversation with our animals that we may not even be recognizing. For example, if in the middle of the day I wonder, Did I remember to hide my slippers? I am under the delusion that my brain has generated this thought. It is more than likely what happened was, as Sasha sat down to devour a slipper, she sent the thought to me, This slipper sure is tasty. Glad you didn't hide it as usual. Or when I start wondering, Is Goldie peeing on my bathmat again?, what's really going on is that Goldie has just sent me this message: I really had to go! I made it to your mat just in time.

Discovering my telepathic abilities would cost me $145 for a one-day workshop. I already had several messages I was eager to deliver, such as: "Dogs who eat slippers end up searching for bunnies in West Virginia," or "No one in the Loire Valley is taking another incontinent cat."

The workshop was held in a meeting room at a Holiday Inn in Maryland. Seated in a circle were fifteen women and one man, between the ages of thirty and fifty-five. There were also four dogs: a hound mix, a Labrador mix, a mostly German shephard, and one shaggy, cat-sized, gray mutt that looked like a prototype for a stuffed animal that never made it into production.

While the dogs wandered the room, Delphine opened with a long spiel about the process of becoming professional animal communicators ourselves, which required signing up for a year's worth of workshops with Delphine.

Next she had us each introduce ourselves and explain why we were here. I was not surprised that there were several single women with what could be considered a surfeit of cats. One said she had fifteen, and she was here because "my feelings overwhelm them." If I was scooping fifteen litter boxes a day, I too would be overwhelmed with my feelings about the cats. Another woman was there because she wanted to express the intensity of her love more directly to her Labrador. I had the feeling that anyone who needed a workshop for this probably had a dog who would like to communicate, "Please, please, leave me alone."

Barbara was a psychologist with ten cats who used them in her practice. She described how at one of her group therapy sessions a man declared he was done with treatment. When one of her cats draped herself on the man's feet and refused to move, Barbara said the man got the cat's message and stayed. (The message I would have gotten was that four hundred years ago this therapist would have been burned at the stake.)

Julie was a dog lover, but because of the rules of her apartment building, she could only have guinea pigs. She took out a thick stack of photographs of them and passed them around the circle. Several people said they'd never seen cuter rodents. Julie had started with a single guinea pig, Russell, who was very content running around his exercise ring and being adored by Julie. Then she added a second guinea pig, Twix, and all hell broke loose. Russell started attacking Twix, and when Julie took him out of his cage to pet him, Russell was cold and distant. She called in an animal communicator to evaluate the situation.

After a few minutes of communication, the communicator told Julie that Russell had spoken to her very clearly. He said, "Do you know there's another guinea pig in my cage?"

Through the communicator Julie tried to explain to Russell that Twix was his new friend. She also told Russell that Twix had been abused in the past. (I wondered what had happened to Twix—could he be a guinea pig who had been used as a guinea pig?) Russell wasn't having any of it. He told Julie back, through the communicator, that he didn't really care about Twix's problems because now Twix was in his cage making his life miserable. Julie said things in the cage were at an impasse and that she was here to learn how to communicate directly with Russell and Twix, since having a communicator on call was prohibitively expensive.

I was up next. I explained that despite making great progress with Sasha, I still felt we could deepen our bond. Specifically it would help if she didn't bolt every time I said, "Come." I also explained how things had degenerated urinewise with the cats.

Then there was Lisa, who was the owner of the four dogs roaming the room. She told about how she was frustrated with her career in retailing and desperately wanted to devote her life to dogs. At her coffee break one day she was sitting in the office kitchenette when her eye was caught by an article about Delphine. She called Delphine from her desk at work and that night she had tickets to California to attend one of Delphine's workshops.

"There are no coincidences," Delphine interjected.

The workshop changed her life. She quit her job and now was on the eve of launching a doggy day care center at her home.

As she spoke her dogs (the hound, Lulu; the Lab, Rex; the German shepherd, Wiley; and the what-is-it, Mugsy) sniffed us, each other, and the snack table. I was impressed with their good behavior. I shuddered at the thought of letting Sasha wander around a hotel conference room. Even though I considered her housebroken, I wouldn't want to test whether she was able to generalize this concept. At that moment Lulu squatted and peed on the carpet. I was stunned. Clearly, Delphine was on to something. The reason I was thinking about my dog peeing on the carpet was that Lulu had sent a message—just to me!—that she was about to take a whiz.

Lisa interrupted her story to reprimand Lulu and take her outside. I did wonder that since Lisa and Lulu should now be in close communication, why Lulu didn't let Lisa know what was about to happen. That thought was interrupted when Wiley, after sniffing around Lulu's accident, himself squatted and made a rather liquid poop on the carpet. Why hadn't Delphine picked up on Wiley's distress and advised Lisa to take Wiley with her?

Delphine began telling us about the essence of telepathic communication while she dabbed gingerly at the mess on the carpet with napkins. She explained that she had no special psychic skills and still doesn't—telepathy is an ability all of us innately have.

We just have to trust our feelings and our intuition. "When your body goes 'unnhh,' trust it." Everyone was nodding madly, but I felt left out. When my body goes "unnhh," it's usually because I've just tried to get into a pair of newly washed jeans.

She said her first experience with telepathic animal communication occurred about twenty years ago when she was a business executive. At about the same time she got a cat and got married and everything was fine, until two years later the cat started soiling all over the house. I sat forward, raptly.

Delphine took the cat to the vet, who checked it out and said everything was fine. He suggested there was probably a psychological problem and referred her to an animal communicator. The communicator came to the house and quickly made a diagnosis. "She said the cat is soiling because there is tension in the marriage. I got a divorce and the cat stopped soiling," Delphine said with a satisfied smile.

I realized I would have a difficult time coming home from the workshop and saying to my husband, "I've got good news and bad news. The good news is there's a way to get Goldie to stop peeing. The bad news is that you need to pack."

After a lunch break, we started the process of tuning into Lisa's dogs. When we came back only Lulu and Rex were left—Lisa had taken Wiley and Musgy home. We began with Lulu. She was a big good-looking dog with a mottled coat of browns and beiges. She seemed to understand it was all about her and happily lay down in the center of the circle of chairs.

Delphine explained that when we began our communication with animals we had to be open to all kinds of messages. Some communicated in images, odd images we would have to interpret. Some animals were extremely verbal. Delphine mentioned one loquacious rabbit she treated who talked so much she had to schedule a second session to hear everything the rabbit wanted to say. We also should know that animals had great senses of humor (I thought Goldie's urinary slapstick was getting somewhat repetitive), and that they had an unerring sense of time. However, Sasha's desire to run into the street if she escaped from her leash demonstrated what I thought was a flawed comprehension of the future.

Delphine advised us to open a session with any animal by asking, "Are you willing to communicate with me?" Once you get the go-ahead, don't conduct an inquisition; better to ask some gentle, open-ended questions such as "Tell me about yourself," or "Share one of your favorite activities."

With that we were ready, all of us, to start a simultaneous dialogue with Lulu. By this time, however, Lulu had fallen deeply asleep and was snoring contentedly. "Being asleep will not affect the quality of the communication," said Delphine, a principle I had put to less than effective use during most college lectures.

We all closed our eyes and concentrated on Lulu. Usually when I have tried to enter quiet, meditative states, I find my mind wandering to such pressing topics as, "Did I pick up the sweater from the dry cleaner?" and "Are we out of soy sauce?" But as I concentrated on the thoughts of the sleeping Lulu, my mind was an utter blank. At first I felt like a failure, then I realized, this may be the mental state of a sleeping hound.

Delphine called us back to attention and asked what we had picked up. "Action" said one woman. "She's confused by the size of her head," said another, "she feels it's too little for her body." "I see swings," said one woman. "Me, too!" said another. Then the therapist spoke. "I think she was an Indian warrior in her previous life. Also a teacher, because I see a middle school. I also see her driving in a car, looking out the window, and the car is smashed."

We were all stunned by Barbara's detail. Unfortunately, Lulu did not rouse herself to confirm or deny any of this. It was my turn. I knew that "Your dog is flat-lining" would not fit the mood of the day. Instead, since Lisa had said all her dogs were rescues, I went with, "She loves you very much and her big concern is having to go back to her previous situation." Both Delphine and Lisa furrowed their brows at this. It turned out, said Lisa, that Lulu's mother was a rescue, but Lulu had been born at Lisa's home.

Lisa explained she was concerned about how her existing dogs were going to adjust to the doggy day care center she was about to open. So we next had to ask Lulu her opinions on that. We all closed our eyes for another five minutes during which—from the answers everybody then gave—Lulu was madly expressing herself to everyone but me. At the end of it Delphine told Lisa that Lulu would be fine, but she needed to be the greeter of other dogs, and she also wanted to have a strict schedule all the dogs had to stick to.

Next was Rex. Rex was not as soporific a subject as Lulu. Lisa had a hard time corralling him into the center of our little circle. Finally he sat and we began our communication. The therapist, Barbara, again had the most complete reading on Rex. "I first saw an eagle feather with a drop of blood on it. That turned into an Indian-head nickel. Next I got an aerial view of a race-track. And I kept seeing teeth. He's very proud of his teeth, he wants everyone to admire them."

I couldn't compete with that, but he seemed like a lively dog and I was determined to say something not completely off the mark. Without ever feeling Rex had whispered in my ear, I settled on the notion that he lived to have fun. "Fun. That's his raison d'être!" I said, to another set of frowns from Lisa and Delphine.

It turned out, Lisa revealed, "Rex bites the other dogs viciously." She held out the inside of her forearm, which had a red, raised scar. "He bit me. But he felt terrible about it afterward." Clearly I was no animal clairvoyant, and clearly Barbara was. Lisa explained that she had found Rex at a highway rest stop when she saw that there was a van there filled with dogs. They were being rescued from a shelter in West Virginia (was West Virginia's major export unbalanced dogs?) and, as she said, "I had to have one."

In the two years Lisa had had Rex, his behavior had gotten worse. "Why does he bite the other dogs? And how can I do doggy day care with him around?" Lisa implored the group. I realized she had a serious problem. It would be hard to say to her customers, "Here's Fifi. Oh, hold on, her back legs are still in the kitchen."

All of us closed our eyes and concentrated on Rex again. After five minutes people had many insights. He needed to sniff flower essences; his chakras were blocked; he had gas. I thought the best solution would be to put him back in a van heading west with a tape of John Denver singing, "Almost heaven, West Virginia . . ."

By then the time had run out. Delphine congratulated us on a fabulous job. "This is telepathy!" she said. She reminded everyone who was going to the next day's advanced workshop to bring photographs of their animals. People would then look at the photo and communicate long distance. "You will find it is easier because you are not reading body language."

"Can we bring pictures of animals who have died?" asked one woman.

Absolutely! Clearly it didn't matter if the animal was asleep, in the room, or even alive. Delphine implied the deader the animal, the better and more pure the communication.

She encouraged us all to exchange phone numbers and e-mails, and to meet once a month to keep up our new telepathic skills. But I slipped out before everyone could read my mind.

*　*　*

Two weeks after my training we had an animal crisis. Things had been quiet with our pets for a while, so we were due. I put the cat food on the kitchen counter (the only place it was safe from Sasha) and noticed that only Biscuit came to haul himself up to eat. I didn't think much of it, but by bedtime I realized Goldie had never shown up at the food bowl. My husband, daughter, and I searched the house. As I climbed the attic stairs I had visions of coming on a scene right out of some Farrelly Brothers movie, in which Goldie, miscalculating his girth, had gotten himself irreparably stuck in the slats of my daughter's disassembled crib. No, he wasn't there. Then, as I descended to the basement, I thought maybe he had tried to hoist himself on a high surface, only to crash disastrously like an obese pole vaulter. But none of us could find him.

After our last visit with the veterinarian, when she said we might have to put the cats outside for part of the day, I had decided that some fresh air and exercise would do them good. While keeping Sasha inside, I put Goldie and Biscuit out back. They sniffed the air curiously for a few minutes, then both ran into the filthy, insect-infested crawl space under the house, like a pair of deposed Iraqi dictators. After a couple of hours I dragged them out and cleaned them up. I tried putting them out the next day, but when I carried them to the door they started crying and scratching me. I gave up.

Where can a fat indoor cat go? We were used to Sasha trying to bolt out the door each time we opened it, but given Goldie's aversion to the outdoors, it seemed impossible he had waddled outside when we weren't noticing. The next morning Goldie didn't appear for breakfast. We were getting alarmed, although we did notice that the mats in the kitchen and bathroom were dry, indicating Goldie truly was gone. I got a photo of Goldie, went to the copy store, and made a bunch of missing-cat posters decorated with hearts. My daughter and I taped them up all over the neighborhood. Several people called to express their condolences, but no one had any news of him. I called the local shelter, but all their recent cat arrivals looked starved.

That night, in bed, my husband and I had the kind of conversation that only can be had under cover of darkness.

"What if Goldie doesn't come back?" I said.

"Then our major animal problem will have been solved," said my husband.

"It was nice not to have to start the day by scrubbing pee out of the den carpet."

"Face it, this is a miracle."

The next morning, when my husband went out to pick up the newspapers, Goldie was on the front steps. He bounded up to his food bowl, nudging Biscuit out of the way.

Although I had been the worst student by far at my telepathy class, I discovered that I had an uncanny ability to hear Goldie's story of his disappearance. Even stranger, though he'd never been out of Washington, D.C., Goldie spoke like a British butler on *Masterpiece Theater*:

"My departure was due to the constant disparagement of both my physique and deportment," he told me in clipped tones. "I didn't see the point of remaining under circumstances in which I was characterized as 'that big hunk of urinating flab.' I decided it was time for me to find a more congenial setting. I slipped out one day when you were preoccupied with trying to restrain that long-eared creature with the repugnant personal habits of whom you seem inordinately fond. Freedom was brilliant, and I would have continued with my new, unencumbered life, but during my peregrinations I noticed that you had festooned my likeness on telegraph poles all over the neighborhood. Although I found the sentimentality of the tiny hearts cloying, I realized my absence was causing you distress, so I concluded I should return. In addition, my bladder was becoming distended due to my inability to procure any carpeting on which to empty it."

Later that morning, when I stepped out of the shower and put my foot on the mat, it landed on a spot still warm from Goldie's latest.

21

NO EXPENSE SPARED

Dogs make you pay and pay and pay.

When I talked to some of my friends about their animals, I realized that as long as I hadn't had to deplete my 401(k) to cover pet-related expenses, I was doing better than they were. Take my Slate colleague Kathleen and her partner, Martha, who live in Seattle. Both women had demanding careers and after much discussion decided they were ready for a dog—a low-maintenance dog. A friend, an emergency room veterinarian, said she'd look for an appropriate dog for them, and soon she said she'd found him: a four-year-old, sixteen-pound Lhasa apso mix named Hank. Only later did Kathleen and Martha realize that a woman who spends her life in the emergency room may have a distorted sense of what normal looks like.

Hank had belonged to an elderly couple who, one after the other, died. The couple had employed a younger couple as caretakers and they wanted to keep Hank. But the family of the deceased couple kicked the younger couple out of the house. The younger couple, with nowhere to go, brought Hank to a shelter.

Kathleen and Martha came to look at Hank. "His face was his most significant feature," said Martha. "He had obviously been hit by a car or something. The right side of his face was collapsed and his right eye was sunken in and not functioning. His left ear stuck out. His bottom teeth also stuck out and were snaggled. He was cute in a messed-up way." They decided to take him. Both women row for exercise so shortly after they got him, they took him with them into the boat. He loved being on the water. However, when they got home the excitement of it all sent him over the edge.

Martha: "He started to stumble."

Kathleen: "Then he collapsed."

Martha: "It was like he was asleep with his eyes open."

The women called their emergency room vet friend—she had been on the rowing outing—and she said she would meet them at the hospital. By the time they arrived Hank was perky again. "This should have given us a clear warning of what we were getting into," said Martha. "But you can't fall in love, then out of love because a dog is inconvenient." Their friend could find no cause for the episode, but suggested they get a regular vet.

The next week they took him in for an evaluation. "That's when the aging process began," said Kathleen. The vet determined Hank was probably six, not four. The vet also detected a heart murmur and suggested they consult a cardiologist.

"I thought, What do you mean, a *cardiologist,*" said Kathleen. "I just wanted a healthy little mutt."

They took him to the cardiologist. "We now have a diagram of his heart chambers and where they're weak," said Kathleen. They left with a bag of medicine for his heart and a much older dog. The cardiologist estimated Hank was eight.

Because of his misshapen face, they kept Hank's bangs long over his bad right eye, but one day he came in from the yard with his good eye scrunched up—he had cut it on something. Off they went to the vet who referred them to the ophthalmologist.

"He upped Hank's age to ten," said Kathleen. "He said he was an old dog with cataracts." They came away with two more medications: antibiotic drops for the cut eye, and gloop they had to squirt in both eyes to keep them moist.

While the eye healed the vet recommended he wear a cone, which the technician tied on Hank with a gauze bow. "He looked just like Little Bo Peep to me," said Martha. "I started laughing so hard I was crying. The tech thought I was hysterical over his condition. She asked me if I was all right, and when I said I was laughing, she recoiled."

Hank wore his Bo Peep collar for most of the rest of his life.

Next, Hank got an infection in his crooked ear. The vet—who remarkably didn't age Hank on this visit—gave them a syringe and bottle of saline. Their job was to warm the saline, draw it into the syringe, and slowly pour it in his ear to drain his infection. "It used to run all over the place," said Martha. They didn't seem to be doing anything wrong, but he could never completely shake the infection.

Kathleen and Martha had always loved to travel, which was why they told their friend they were looking for an easy dog, not one who required the services of the Mayo Clinic. Still, they were determined not to become housebound because of Hank. So when they went away, they hired a team: a house sitter, and an elder-care dog sitter. By this time they had had Hank for a little over a year, and not only was he mostly blind, he was completely deaf. This caused problems for the various dog sitters they employed, all of whom would arrive, and finding Hank asleep and unresponsive to noise, would assume he was dead. "One told me she poked him with a pencil," said Kathleen.

When Kathleen and Martha returned from a ten-day vacation,

they were alarmed at Hank's rapid decline. Because of his ear problem, he had lost his balance, and turned in circles, or walked against the wall to stay upright. They started taking him to his doctors weekly. "One time the vet just said, 'We won't charge you for this visit,'" said Kathleen. They got a baby gate to keep him from going up the stairs, but when he was upstairs one day, he miscalculated the first step and fell down the whole flight.

"I was there," said Kathleen. "I was so upset, I heard him falling. He was just a little clump at the bottom of the stairs, a bag of bones." They took him to the vet who said he had only bruised himself, but they all agreed he was miserable and the time to end it was drawing near. The vet also concluded Hank was twelve years old.

Martha, who had recently left her job, decided to stay home with Hank for the last months to care for him.

Martha: "I would sit on the sofa and watch *Emergency Vets* on Animal Planet and hold Hank and cry. I would watch all these sad stories and I knew what was coming."

Kathleen: "I would call her and say, 'Turn off *Emergency Vets*!'"

Finally, they made his final vet appointment. On his last night they gave him his favorite meal of grilled chicken and took him for a tiny walk in the park. "He was such a sweet dog," said Kathleen. "He was a sweetie through everything." They had Hank for only eighteen months, during which they spent $6,000, and he aged eight years.

My friend Jane incurred plenty of veterinarian bills during the sixteen years she had her yellow Lab, Peaches. But closing in on that expense were the costs of redecorating due to the undiscriminating nature of Peaches' palate. The members of the Donner Party were pickier eaters than Peaches.

Peaches was the senior dog in Jane's household—it was my

daughter's cuddling of their yellow Lab puppy Dugan that caused us to get Sasha, who for me launched a thousand trips to the vet.

Jane first noticed Peaches had a problem when she and her husband, Bill, moved from Washington, D.C., to Santa Monica, California. Peaches loved to roam the hillside of their property, and although she was getting more exercise than she ever had, after a few months she began looking like a sausage about to burst its casing. Jane and Bill were baffled as to the cause until the day they walked up the hill and discovered at the foot of an avocado tree a huge pile of skins and pits. They realized Peaches was eating about a dozen avocados a day. Despite her obesity, they had to admit her diet was giving her an amazingly lustrous coat.

Jane had an infant daughter and was working at home. With the discovery of Peaches' love of avocados, Jane divided her time among caring for the baby, trying to work, and listening for the sound of falling fruit. As she heard each thwack, she raced Peaches up the hill, trying to get to the guacamole first.

When the family returned to Washington, D.C., their regular vet ordered that Peaches had to reduce. Her meals now came from a bag of prescription low-cal dog food. "Given how much it cost, I thought it should be made of Beluga caviar," said Jane. "I read the label and we were feeding her the world's most expensive peanut shells."

This made Peaches desperately hungry, so she roved the house looking to supplement her diet. She particularly liked the cuisine in the bathroom. Peaches ate a tube of toothpaste, a box of cold lozenges, half a package of chocolate Ex-Lax. When they had overnight guests, Jane and Bill warned them to keep all their bags zipped and their toiletries out of reach, as if guarding against marauding wildlife in a national park.

Special occasions were particularly special for Peaches. She ate their daughter's entire second-birthday cake. "The cake was on the counter and we went for a walk. When we came back all that was left were the candles," said Jane. "It was the only time in her life she looked truly blissed out. It was the meal she'd been dreaming of." Their daughter's third birthday passed without incident, which led them to drop their guard. The following year, Peaches ate their daughter's fourth-birthday cake.

One year Peaches ate all of their daughter's Halloween candy, an entire grocery bag full. All that was left were a few crinkled wrappers and broken lollipop sticks. Peaches vomited most of it. That Christmas Jane and her daughter had lovingly decorated a large gingerbread house, complete with frosting snow and a peppermint candy pathway. Peaches devoured it, then regurgitated it in the form of orange goo all over the tan carpet in the family room. They spent $700 to replace the rug.

There was the morning Jane came down to find Peaches flat on the kitchen floor moaning in agony. Jane, who only had about twenty pounds on Peaches, wrestled the dog into the car and took her to the vet. After an initial exam the vet said it looked like Peaches was dying of a tumor. "I said to the vet, 'I'm sure she's eaten something,'" recalled Jane. No, it's probably cancer, said the vet. Although Jane had never spent a day at veterinary school, the X-ray showed her diagnosis was correct.

There was an enormous blockage in Peaches' stomach. Without surgery Peaches would die an agonizing death. With surgery, Jane would end up with an elderly dog—Peaches was now eleven years old—and a whopping bill. "She's staring at me, and it's thumbs-up or thumbs-down time," said Jane. Peaches looked at Jane begging for another chance. Jane let them operate.

The surgeon removed a huge T-bone, still wrapped in a garbage bag, which had been thrown out after the previous night's steak dinner. The bill, including a four-day hospital stay with IV, came to $3,500.

Jane and Bill needed a break from guarding against Peaches' binge-and-purge episodes, so the family went to the Bahamas for a long weekend. The ideal person to look after Peaches would be a retired Secret Service agent who'd served on the presidential detail, but the best they could do was to pay for twenty-four-hour coverage with the two shifts of dog sitters. Before Jane and Bill left they swept the house for anything ingestible, and went off with a clear conscience.

It turned out they had forgotten to dispose of the mesh bag of onions in the pantry and a larger-than-life papier-mâché sculpture of a cat made by their eight-year-old daughter. Onions and papier-mâché cats are hard on the digestive system. They returned to find Peaches had left the downstairs covered with a layer of vomit and excrement. The only economical thing to do was cover their wall-to-wall carpet with area rugs. Since Peaches liked to scoot around on her rear end to wipe herself, those too soon were stained.

After this Jane and Bill realized they could never leave Peaches alone for an extended period—or a short one. They decided as long as Peaches was around, they could only go on vacations within driving distance. So one of them drove Peaches to their destination, while the other flew there with their daughter. On a trip to Vermont it was Jane's turn to take Peaches. She plotted a roundabout route based on hotels that allowed dogs (for an extra fee, of course).

When they traveled together Jane always booked a room with two beds. On their way to Vermont they stopped at a lovely hotel in Providence, Rhode Island, that provided two queen beds with piles of feather pillows and a thick down comforter. Jane helped Peaches get up and bid her good night. In the morning when Jane looked over at her companion, Peaches was draped across her own bed, stretching languorously. Peaches' thoughts couldn't have been clearer: "After all these years, you finally understand how to treat me."

By age twelve, Peaches was fading, so Jane and Bill decided to inject some youthful energy into their household. Welcome, Dugan. Dugan not only changed my life, he changed those of Jane, Bill, and Peaches. Peaches was like a CEO who names a replacement only to realize, "Hey, I'm still in the prime of life and that snot-nose is not taking over this company." She was immediately revived by Dugan's arrival. Dugan had so much youthful energy that he reminded Jane and Bill that it had been nine years since they'd had to get up repeatedly in the night with a hungry, wet baby.

About eight months after Dugan arrived, Jane got a notice to move her car off the street because new asphalt was going to be laid. As the trucks rumbled through the neighborhood, spewing hot tar, Peaches and Dugan went insane with excitement. Jane was marooned in the house with them, trying to figure out how to get to her car, now parked a block away, without getting trapped in the goo. To survey the situation she opened the front door. In an instant, Dugan shot down the walk and into the wet, tarry street.

Liberated, he decided to visit the Labrador who lived across the way. Jane screamed his name until she was hoarse; he was oblivious. She realized she too would have to traipse across the muck and retrieve her retriever. She put on a pair of old shoes. "It was like walking on bubble gum on a hot day," she said. By the time she got hold of Dugan, his paws were clotted islands of tar; it was wedged up between the webbing in his formerly pink pads. His stomach, flanks, and private parts were splattered black. He was more spotted on his underbelly than a Dalmatian.

He was also wildly prancing and leaping, eager to put his filthy black paws on Jane. Using bullfighter maneuvers, she managed to avoid a direct hit, but as she pivoted she saw, to her horror, that Dugan was heading up the front walk toward the house.

The event has been memorialized as real estate artwork. Paw-shaped indentations decorate the street in front of the house, which turn into black paw patterns dancing up the bluestone walk, and continue up the porch steps to the front door. Jane got her tar puppy out back and called the vet on the cell phone. He suggested calling the poison control center, for advice on how to detar. A very expensive ophthalmologic ointment is the best solvent, the woman at poison control advised.

Dugan was now huge and adolescent, so adolescent that he sprouted a snoutful of acne. Off they went to the vet, and Jane returned home with a tube of canine pimple cream. By this time, Peaches was fifteen and on the decline. When I visited Jane's house Peaches was lying on the kitchen floor, her droopy, red-rimmed eyes giving her a woeful look. Whenever Jane spoke to her she would try to get up, but she moved with the awkwardness of a seal negotiating an ice floe.

Jane recognized it was time to send the ice floe holding Peaches out to sea, but had been unable to do it. Because Peaches insisted on sleeping with them, her husband carried the eighty-pound dog up the stairs each night. "It's actually better than doing biceps curls at the gym," he said. Things continued to slide. Peaches began to wake them up at five A.M. not because she had to go outside to relieve herself, but just to let them know she had already relieved herself. Amazingly, at Thanksgiving she managed to rouse herself for one more household-pillaging mission and devoured much of the turkey carcass with explosive results.

Jane made the appointment for the final appointment. But when Jane got to the vet's office she found out that the five stages of grief would be delayed due to the invoking of the veterinarian code. The code consists of this question: You don't want to euthanize your dog if she can be kept alive by spending a lot of money, do you? Jane agreed to shots to help activate Peaches' back legs, and a bagful of pills to revive Peaches' failing systems. The vet also showed Jane how to use a bath towel like a winch across Peaches' midsection so that Jane could give herself sciatica by hauling Peaches in and out of the house.

This went on for months. Finally, even the vet conceded sixteen years was all Peaches was going to get, and they put her down. Jane was devastated. "It's a real downside of owning a dog," she said. "They don't live long enough."

At least Jane happily, more or less, laid out her money for dog maintenance. This was not the case in the matter of Pipsie. My friend Jon called me one day and said, "I was just talking to a friend in New York, and I have a dog story for you." Jon's friend David was a thirty-something Manhattan executive dating another thirty-something Manhattan executive, Jennifer. Jennifer was about to find out that she and David diverged on their view of how well their relationship was going.

For the couple of months they'd been together, David had developed an increasing intolerance, which now bordered on disgust, toward Jennifer's Yorkshire terrier, Pipsie. Pipsie weighed about six pounds and was the size of a football. She was so much like a football that Jennifer liked to toss her in the air in a game of catch. But no football had long silky hair that was put up in pink bows; owners of footballs did not speak to them in baby talk.

David was fastidious, and he was getting sick of picking Pipsie's long hairs off his suits. He was getting sick of being pushed to the corner of the bed so Pipsie could cuddle with Jennifer. Most of all, he was sick of watching Jennifer kiss Pipsie, then having to kiss Jennifer himself.

It was a Thursday evening, and he and Jennifer had dinner

plans. David decided before they went out he would go to Jennifer's apartment and break the news that they were breaking up. Besides being fastidious, he was also cheap. He thought if he got it over with in Jennifer's apartment, he could avoid a dinner bill. They had a glass of wine, and he gingerly approached the subject. He wasn't sure Jennifer understood where the conversation was going when she got up to excuse herself for a minute. While he was waiting for Jennifer, David picked up the newspaper and began reading. Pipsie thought it was a game and started jumping and hitting the newspaper. David shooed her away, but Pipsie kept coming. Finally, David saw Pipsie was poised at his feet, ready to make a leap for the paper. To teach her a lesson, at the moment she did, he yanked it away.

Pipsie crashed headfirst into David's knee, let out a high-pitched yelp, and fell to the floor. Was she dead or just unconscious? Here he was trapped in a scene right out of *There's Something About Mary*. As he tried to remember how Matt Dillon revived the dead dog in that movie, Jennifer returned. She didn't seem to appreciate this amazing film homage taking place in her living room.

"What did you do to Pipsie!" she shrieked.

"Nothing," said David. "She was coming at me and I just moved out of the way." He wondered how Pipsie's apparent demise was going to affect his breakup plans.

Jennifer, weeping, picked up the dog and began performing mouth-to-snout resuscitation. That's it, thought David. I am never kissing this woman again. After a few minutes, Pipsie, weak and dazed, regained consciousness. Jennifer grabbed her coat and David. They ran out through the lobby and Jennifer hailed a cab. She gave the address of the nearest animal hospital. During the cab ride Jennifer, gasping between sobs, continued with her mouth-to-snout. They arrived at the hospital, a large, swanky building. When they got to the front desk, the receptionist said the hospital required a $500 deposit to admit the dog. Jennifer looked at David. He took out his American Express card. Pipsie was whisked away. After an hour in the waiting room, listening to Jennifer's weeping, David suggested they go to dinner. She refused—to his relief. He took a cab home.

The next morning Jennifer, who had spent the night at the hospital, called with the news. Pipsie was on life support, but had been stabilized. She was in a semiprivate room. David said he hated to ask, at a time like this and all, but what exactly did doggy life support in a semiprivate room in Midtown Manhattan cost?

"Four hundred and seventy-five dollars a day," she replied.

And how long would Pipsie need to be hospitalized? Jennifer hung up on him.

He called his friends for advice. How long after Pipsie's recovery or death would he have to wait to finish breaking up with Jennifer? And how did he get the bill transferred off his American Express card? His friends were generally unsympathetic.

Pipsie spent the weekend, and was discharged Monday. She was functioning but fragile. More robust was the bill. It came to $1,200.

David went to Jennifer's apartment to finish his breakup conversation. He got no argument that their relationship was through. He got no argument about the bill, either. She was firm that he could keep it—he could even think of it as a parting gift from Pipsie.

22

GOING FOR BROKE

Disability by dog.

For years my friend Bonnie had a string of dogs who had a propensity for trouble. But like many hard-core dog people, she had ready excuses for their deficiencies (dog people, I noticed, tended to have a more objective view of their children than of their dogs) and trouble letting go. Take her dog, Coco, her springer spaniel mix, who once, by hitting the automatic lock button in the Plymouth Valiant, managed to lock herself, the keys, and Bonnie's purse in the car when Bonnie stepped away after double-parking in rush hour traffic in downtown Washington, D.C.

By the time Coco was fifteen she was incontinent, falling down the stairs, deaf and blind. But Bonnie couldn't bring herself to end it. Then Bonnie was diagnosed with breast cancer. She knew that during her treatments she wouldn't have the strength or energy to deal with Coco, who followed her constantly, whimpering. The day Bonnie started chemo, her husband, Jim, took Coco to be put down.

"That was her last man's-best-friend act for me, to let me cry for her, because I hadn't let myself cry over the cancer," said Bonnie.

Bonnie recovered completely in a dogless house. For four years they went without a dog, to Jim's delight. Bonnie had to acknowledge it was a relief to be able to go on vacations without having to make elaborate dog-sitting plans, or to spend the day away without having to run home because the dog was in the yard and it was raining. Then it started gnawing at her: She needed a dog.

Actually, she wanted a dog for her young son, Nathan, who had shown a total indifference to the idea. He wanted a cat, which was impossible because Jim was allergic. Bonnie tried to subtly indoctrinate her son into the glories of dog ownership, but it was like trying to convince him to take up needlepoint. Then one day, in response to one of her brainwashing sessions, he said, "I guess a dog would maybe be fun. Sort of." At that Bonnie put him in the car and they drove to a nearby animal shelter.

In a cage in the basement was a five-month-old golden retriever mix. Neighbors had noticed he was being abused and reported him to animal control. Bonnie asked if they could pat the dog. The cage was opened and Nathan went in and put his arms around the dog's neck. "The dog wasn't very well behaved, he was barking and barking, but he had a sweet face," said Bonnie. She put in an application and brought the dog home a few days later. They named him Jack.

Jim was resigned to Jack's presence; Nathan was intermittently interested; Bonnie was thrilled. Jack quickly reached his full size of seventy pounds. Bonnie, a runner and long-distance biker, loved having a dog to keep her company on her workouts. But she knew this was a new era of leash laws and that Jack couldn't follow her unrestrained.

One day Bonnie went for a long bike ride with Jack running alongside her. Her destination was a wooded trail where she could take him off the leash. But first they had to pass by a park and playground. As they got to the playground Bonnie wrapped the leash around her hand. Jack had never bothered a child, but because he was so big she didn't want to run the risk.

It was a glorious day. Bonnie was peddling, listening to music in her headphones, when she felt a tug on the leash. Out of the corner of her eye she saw that Jack had spotted a squirrel. There had been many squirrels along the way, but this was the first to light a fire in Jack's soul. He only hesitated a second, long enough for Bonnie to scream, "Jack, NO!" before he took off. "I could have let go of the leash, but I didn't because I didn't want him to go after any people."

Bonnie held tight as seventy pounds of dog pulled her onto the concrete. This did not immediately deter Jack's pursuit. He dragged Bonnie across the pavement until he realized she wasn't being much fun. He circled back and stood over her, nudging her with his nose.

Bonnie was facedown. She tasted blood. She moved her tongue around and thought she had pebbles in her mouth until she realized the pellets were her teeth. She gingerly moved all her limbs. Her left leg indicated it would be best to stop moving it.

She became aware there were people around her. She realized the man calling out, "Ma'am?" was talking to her. "Ma'am, I can't get closer to you because your dog won't let me," he said. Bonnie heard Jack barking as one of the men said he was calling 911. Still facedown she gave them Jim's number.

"When the ambulance guys came there was more discussion about the dog because no one could get near me," Bonnie recalled. Finally, Bonnie heard Jim call to her and she let go of the leash. "Everyone was saying, 'Whoa, she's letting go,'" Bonnie said. Jack immediately ran to Jim, who was not thrilled to see that Jack was somehow implicated in his wife's being facedown on the sidewalk with an ambulance waiting.

Jim took Jack home and met Bonnie at the hospital. The top of her tibia was crushed; her leg was broken in twenty-seven places. The surgeon said putting it back together was like sculpting with potato chips. With enough screws and metal plates he made a functioning leg. After more than a week in the hospital Bonnie was discharged. The surgeon wanted to give her a soft cast, but Bonnie insisted on plaster. "I was a little afraid of Jack," Bonnie said. "He loves me so much and is so enthusiastic, I was afraid he would bump me." She was also slightly afraid Jim would want to bump him off. But Bonnie never blamed Jack. "I knew he wasn't smart to begin with," she said. "It was my fault." She was surprised at how many visitors, once they saw Bonnie was all right, asked, "And how's Jack?"

"He didn't get the squirrel," Bonnie replied.

Eventually Bonnie's leg healed. Jack got some obedience training and now responds to basic commands. Things got back to normal. Jim tolerates Jack, Nathan occasionally pays some attention, Bonnie loves him.

Another friend, Amy, had a childhood dog who had passive-aggressive problems. That is, the dog was passive when it needed to be aggressive and aggressive when it needed to be passive. Amy grew up on a farm in upstate New York with cows, thirteen cats, and a border collie named Tippy. Amy's father ran a somewhat haphazard dairy operation and Tippy was his working dog, there to herd the herd. But Amy's father hadn't properly trained Tippy, and only put him to work with the cows intermittently. Since Tippy's instinctive desire to herd was unsatisfied, he had to find a way to fulfill it. He chose cars. At the approach of any car or truck, Tippy would dash into the road, like a suicidal traffic cop. "You'd scream at him then watch him roll beneath the under-carriage," recalled Amy. Amazingly, he never got badly hurt.

Because Tippy was so neurotic and hypervigilant, he was an excellent watchdog, but there was very little call for this on their remote farm. "He would bark at phantom burglers," said Amy. Tippy slept on the floor of her parents' bedroom and was constantly waking them with barked alerts in the middle of the night to signal them that nothing was happening.

Once, at three A.M., deep in winter after a mammoth snowstorm, the family was awakened. Not, as usual, by Tippy, but by the sounds of tires spinning ever deeper into snow. Amy's father realized the sounds were coming from their yard. He quickly surmised what was going on: Someone was breaking into the barn. How was it that Tippy hadn't alerted them?

Amy's father jumped up, and in the dark ran across the bedroom to reach for his shotgun. In doing so, he tripped over the sleeping Tippy. Tippy was fine, but Amy's father severely sprained his ankle. Despite Amy's father's tumble, and the subsequent swearing, Tippy remained silent. Amy's father hobbled out back with the gun. There he confronted a group of young thieves who had loaded so much equipment from the barn into the back of their pickup truck that it was now hopelessly jammed in a snowdrift. Tippy finally made it out back, and cowered by his master's damaged foot, watching as the thieves unloaded the equipment so they could get their truck off the property. "My father was furious at Tippy," said Amy. "The incident totally changed their relationship. My father thought he had a working dog, but after that there was no pretense that Tippy was earning his keep." Tippy lived out the rest of his long life as a car-chasing pet.

23

ALL EXPENSE SPARED

Dog owning, the old-fashioned way.

One Sunday, my friend Cindy, owner of the lifesaving Lhasa apso, Cinnamon, came over with her family for brunch. Seeing Sasha swept her with a wave of nostalgia. As a girl in rural Pennsylvania her father, a railroad conductor, supplemented his income by breeding beagles as hunting dogs. Cindy's father wasn't interested in conformation, or bloodlines, or temperament. He had two requirements for the beagles he bred: that the male have the ability to mount and impregnate the female; and that the female be able to bear a litter of puppies.

Until they were old enough to train, Cindy was in charge of the puppies, who lived in a makeshift kennel on the back of the property constructed from boards and wire. The training was to the point. Her father caught a rabbit, sent the beagles running after it, then blew away the rabbit with a shotgun. The shotgun was not only the primary training device, it was also the family's main veterinary tool. "If a dog got sick, my father gave it worming medication," she said. "If it got really sick, he shot it. He wasn't going to pay money for a vet.'"

Many beagles passed through the kennel, but two stuck around for a while, Lucky and Lady. Lucky was terrified of lightning. One time—violating all of Cindy's father's rules about the nature of the human-dog relationship—the family brought Lucky inside the house as they were leaving for church because a storm was coming in. When they returned the curtains had been torn off the walls, the house completely pulled apart. A few storms later Lucky, left outside in her pen, got so agitated she managed to hook her collar on a stake and hang herself. "We always wondered if it was suicide," Cindy said. This story put a damper on the merriment at the brunch table, but then I asked Cindy about Lady.

She said that Lady, perhaps trying to avoid Cindy's father's medical technique, escaped and joined a pack of wild dogs that roamed the area. The rest of the pack stayed far away from people, but Lady still had some residual affection for Cindy's family, so at night she would go from house to house taking things off neighbors' porches—boots, balls, rugs—and drop them on Cindy's porch. This became hugely embarrassing for Cindy's parents. Each day they had to sort out whose stuff they had gotten, and the neighbors looked skeptical when Cindy's parents said it was the dog who was a kleptomaniac.

Finally Cindy's father had had enough. "I was about ten years old, and Lady wouldn't come near anybody but me," she said. "My father told me to stand in the backyard and call her. So I did. She came within about forty feet of me and my father shot her." Forks dropped, and the other guests said it was time they got going. It was like being invited to a dinner theater by friends and finding out that the musical was *Sweeney Todd,* the story of the demon barber who slashed his clients' throats then made them into meat pies.

I asked Cindy how traumatized she had been. "I don't

remember it being a trauma. But I don't remember much of my childhood, and I do remember that." Then she thought of an encore. Strays were constantly passing by her house—Cindy made it sound like the Appalachian Trail for dogs—and as long as they seemed tame Cindy's parents let her keep them. One in particular Cindy adored, a Chihuahua she named Tiny. A little while after Cindy adopted her, Tiny started blowing up, and began looking like a Chihuahua with a German shepherd inside trying to get out. She was. Tiny had mated with some huge passing stranger and was gestating his gigantic puppies. Actually, puppy. There was only room for one, since it was almost as big as Tiny. The puppy was born dead. "Tiny was so badly damaged by the birth that my father shot her," said Cindy. By this time I felt as if I should have handed out Valium instead of bagels at this brunch.

The shots from Cindy's stories were still ringing in my ears when a few days later I ran into my neighbor David. David worked nights, so he often saw me during the day on my innumerable walks with Sasha. He never failed to shake his head in disbelief at how dedicated I was to Sasha's bladder.

It was with even more disbelief that I saw David was holding a leash, on the end of which was White Fang. It was a big creature with Arctic-ready white-gray fur, a long snout, bushy tail, and striking, mismatched eyes—one brown, one blue, as if it couldn't decide which color of contact lenses was most dramatic. This dog looked so much like a wolf that it struck in me an ancient chord of fear and fascination.

"What is going on, David?" I asked.

"Oh, this is Brevard," he said. "He belongs to friends and we agreed to keep him while they're on vacation."

"Brevard is scary-looking," I said.

"Oh, he's a gentle giant," said David, the recent dog cynic, patting Brevard.

"He looks like a wolf, what is he?" I asked.

"I think he was a stray. Come over next Tuesday and ask our friends when they pick him up."

I did. It was odd sitting in a room chatting, drinking wine, while my limbic system kept screaming, "There's a wolf in here!"

Eleven years ago Jim was a college student living in the little town of Brevard, North Carolina. He was renting a cottage next door to a family who were not charter members of People for the Ethical Treatment of Animals. Their white German shepherd spent her days tied with a rope to a tree in the yard. "She was a supersweet dog," recalled Jim. "Even though the kids would tease her and throw things at her and other dogs would come and menace her." She got pregnant—maybe the father was a passing husky, Jim speculated—and gave birth at the tree. She died shortly afterward of a worm infestation. The family got rid of all the puppies, except the most striking one. Apparently believing a tree doesn't look right without a dog tied to it, they attached the puppy with the same rope to the same tree. Again, Jim watched as the children taunted him with sticks and passing dogs snapped. The lonely puppy, left without shelter, howled all night. So some evenings, after the family's lights went out, Jim brought the puppy into his house. He secretly named him Brevard, and kept Brevard with him until dawn, when he returned the poor thing to the tree.

Brevard grew quickly, reaching about eighty-five pounds, with an amazing, thick coat that hung almost to the ground. It was Christmas and Jim was finished with school. He couldn't bear the thought of leaving Brevard to the same fate as his mother. The day of his departure he packed his Buick Regal: "I filled it with everything I own, but left a small spot in the front seat." In the spot he placed a Gaines Burger. At five A.M. he went to the tree, untied Brevard and led him to the car. Brevard hopped into his spot, ate the Gaines Burger, and spent the rest of the four-hour ride to Jim's parents' house with his snout stuck in Jim's ear. When Jim brought Brevard into the house he took one look at the Christmas tree, lifted his leg and relieved himself. It was the only time he went in the house.

"Since then I've never had a problem with him," said Jim. "Taking him was the best decision I ever made." Brevard smacked his tail on the floor in agreement.

24

CANINE CANDY STRIPER

Sasha makes a contribution.

Once, watching my daughter skip down the street, I wondered when I had stopped skipping. You don't decide not to skip ever again, it's just something you realize later that you don't do anymore. As Sasha went through her paces at Todd's class, I saw that without my being aware of it, Sasha had stopped being an untrained dog. She didn't go on the carpet anymore, she came into my office to let me know she had to go out. I could take her for walks and she sat at the curb while we waited to cross. She didn't spend her days fluttering from room to room, as if she was a character in a Tennessee Williams play searching for her departed youth. She staked out a few favorite places to sleep. When she was feeling energetic, she brought us stuffed animals we kept in a basket to toss to her.

Sasha had made so much progress that one day in class Todd said, "She's ready to become certified as a service dog. I work with a group that brings dogs into nursing homes and I think she'd be good at that." It was like turning the page of a baby book and finding the chapter after "Toilet Training" was "Getting a Driver's License."

"I don't think Sasha is therapy-dog material," I said.

"You're wrong. She's actually a very good beagle. I've known so many crazy beagles, but Sasha could do this," he said. "It would be good for her. Dogs like having jobs." Making Sasha a good role model for our daughter cinched it. I contacted the organization People Animals Love and filled out their application, including a character reference for Sasha from the vet. Sasha and I were notified we were approved to go to a training/evaluation session in a meeting room at the National Cathedral, the magnificent Episcopal cathedral where so many dignitaries are eulogized.

With trepidation I walked her to the cathedral grounds, then to the door of the room filled with dogs. Sasha's usual greeting to passing dogs was to pull on her leash and bark fiercely. She particularly liked to do this with dogs at least triple her size. I kept trying to explain to her that it didn't make her seem fierce, it just made her seem like a noisy appetizer. Then there was the house-training issue. Sasha hadn't had an accident in months, but I worried that the pressure of the moment might test her control. I dreaded having to ask the bishop of Washington if he had any enzyme spray in his cassock.

We walked in, and instead of barking at the twenty or so dogs in the room—everything from a Weimaraner, to a bichon frise, to a Cavalier King Charles, to a bulldog, to a mutt with a Mohawk clip—Sasha curled her tail under her and stood near me. Then I saw Todd who came over to say hello. Sasha immediately sat. We were told to grab some chairs and watch a video about PALS. I sat down and Sasha hopped into my lap, resting her head in the crook of my elbow. She had never been so affectionate.

The video almost killed me. It opened with a scene in a nursing home with a dog visiting an elderly man confined to bed. A dog came over and the man immediately became animated, talking to the dog with delight. The man looked like a twin of my late grandfather, the Boston terrier breeder, whom I adored. I choked up and held Sasha closer. Then the film cut to a scene at a children's hospital. The kids, many bald from chemotherapy, were petting dogs. One mother described how she couldn't get her child out of bed until a dog came to visit. Then the girl got into her wheelchair and held on to the dog's leash while the dog pulled her down the hall and she laughed. By this time, Sasha was soaked with my tears.

The head of the organization told us about our duties and responsibilities. I was unable to hear most of what she said because the obese bulldog behind me fell asleep. It snored like a bulldozer, interrupted by sporadic bursts of sleep apnea that sound like engine backfire.

Next, we were told to form ourselves into small groups and role-play a nursing home visit. As I stood up with Sasha several people came over to me to remark on her. "What a well-behaved dog." "How did you train her?" "I thought beagles were supposed to be difficult." We went over to a PALS volunteer who was pretending to be an old person in a wheelchair. I lifted Sasha up and she let herself be stroked.

She wasn't enjoying the event, merely tolerating it. I wondered if I was exploiting my dog by making her become a service dog. Then I thought, am I exploiting my daughter by making her go to school instead of letting her watch television all day? It wouldn't hurt Sasha to become a contributing member of society.

To get certified we had to visit a nursing home just a few blocks away from my house. I had walked by it many times, hoping I would never have a reason to go inside. We waited in the lobby with half a dozen volunteers and dogs, including Todd and his rottweiler, Morgan. How did Sasha know not to bark at the other dogs? To my astonishment she sat quietly by me, provoking more remarks among the dog owners about how well trained she was. I indicated Todd and said, "It's because of him." Todd said, "I told you she could do this."

We set off to the wards. Most of the patients were in wheel-chairs, and I held Sasha up to them to make it easier for them to pat her soft head and ears. Each person I visited had a dog memory: a beloved dog from childhood, or one left behind when the nursing home became home. "Oh, that's a hound dog! I know a hound dog when I see one!" said one woman who described growing up in the country with a father who bred hunting dogs.

The visit was supposed to last an hour, but after forty-five min-utes I could see Sasha couldn't take much more. It wasn't that she whined, or pulled against me on the leash, I could just tell that she'd had enough. I thought how amazing it was that she had gone from a terrified sticklike creature to one whose thoughts I understood. We left and when we got to our front door Sasha ran in and collapsed on the couch for the rest of the day. "Welcome to the working world," I said to her prostrate body.

Although Sasha and I were getting closer, I knew she was lonely for dog companionship and confused by the serial disappearance of her foster buddies. I decided to try turning the relationship between Sasha and the cats from nonrecognition to full diplo-matic exchange. My method was to again put the cats outside during the day. This would give them physical and mental stimu-lation, and an opportunity to pee al fresco. I also hoped that when all three found themselves on the same fenced patio, Sasha could prod them into playing with her, like a camp counselor helping the fat kids get into shape.

As the cats tentatively made their way around the yard, Sasha appeared overjoyed. She ran over to Goldie and showed him how to have a good time. First she gently bit his head, as she had

Roscoe's, Maggie's, and Annie's, to initiate a session of chase. Goldie recoiled and hissed. Ignoring this, Sasha ran a demonstration course. She jumped off the stone wall, ran around the dogwood, and did a figure eight around the bushes. She looked at Goldie as if to say, "Did you get that?" Goldie remained impassive, so patiently, Sasha ran it again. "See, see, down this wall, around here—don't fall into the bush, that's the tricky part!—then back to where we started. Then I'll bite your head again and we'll fall down and bark. It's really fun. Let's go!"

Sasha went over and tried to bite Goldie's head. He swiped at her with his paw. Still she ran the course again and came back to Goldie, only this time staying a foot away from him. Goldie folded up his paws and settled into the mulch. Sasha again barked at him, this time in frustration, and wandered away.

Goldie's reaction reminded me of a commentary I'd read about a recent study on comparative animal intelligence. Harvard graduate student Brian Hare demonstrated that dogs were better than chimpanzees at reading human nonverbal clues. He and colleagues put out two containers, hid food in one, then indicated with looks and gestures (the food couldn't be seen or smelled) which container had the food. The chimpanzees had no idea what the experimenters were going on about; the dogs went for the food. When you think about it, it shouldn't be surprising. Besides Bonzo, over the millennia few chimps have had to learn to please humans in order to get a reliable source of food and a cozy bed. In an article about the study, writer and animal expert Stephen Budiansky pointed out a fact that intrigued me even more than the dog/chimp findings: It is almost impossible to devise a test to measure cat intelligence.

Cats just don't care enough about rewards, which makes it difficult for scientists to determine how smart they are. I thought it was a sign of genius that they understood people so well: "Yeah, yeah, if I do the trick, you'll feed me. But guess what? If I lie here long enough napping and grooming myself, eventually you'll still feed me."

That attitude seemed to be behind Goldie's message to Sasha: "Your routine sure looks like a lot of 'fun.' Just leave me out of it."

Feeling sorry for Sasha, I went outside and clapped and yelled for her as she made her circuit at potentially lethal speed. She seemed so proud that she could instantly vary her course, never once stepping on the plants, never smashing her head against the fence. Maybe she would like agility training, the sport in which a dog runs a circuit of obstacles. I thought of the scene in the wonderful documentary about the national spelling bee, *Spellbound,* in which a mother goes to pick up her appealingly goofy young son, only to find out he's entered himself in the local spelling bee, and not only has he won, he turns out to be a spelling whiz kid. Maybe I had discovered Sasha's hidden talent. I looked up agility clubs in my area. Most of them were hours away; the nearest one had a year-long waiting list. How could getting your dog into a place that teaches it to run around poles be harder than getting your child into college?

I called a local agility judge listed on the American Kennel Club Web site to see if he had any advice. He wasn't very encouraging. He said agility was so popular that there was nothing to do but wait. When I told him I had a beagle, he indicated the wait might not be worthwhile. "I've been an obedience judge for thirty-two years and you don't see too many high-scoring beagles," he said. "There was one beagle at an all-beagle show who was head and shoulders above all the others. Then he thought he saw someone he knew in the audience and ran out of the ring and jumped in that person's lap." I decided to stick to having Sasha run around the backyard.

25

"IS THAT A BANANA IN YOUR POCKET?"

The sniffer dogs of Homeland Security.

Because I live in Washington, D.C., I sometimes hear F-16 fighter jets patrolling the sky at night; my husband and I think of the pilots as the Little Prince. During the anthrax scare, my mail carrier handed me the mail wearing rubber gloves, which I received with my ungloved hands. I now think of suicide-bomber barricades ringing federal buildings as an architectural detail. But the first time I really worried about my safety was when I discovered beagles are employed by the Department of Homeland Security.

If you've ever returned from an international flight, you may have encountered one of these long-eared civil servants; there are seventy such teams patrolling twenty-one international airports. The Beagle Brigade is with the Customs and Border Protection Division of the department. A beagle and a human officer work as a team to prevent contaminated produce or meat from entering the country. Though most violators are travelers who have forgotten they still have an apple in their carry-on, these days the department is also looking out for the possibility of agricultural terrorism, the deliberate introduction of a devastating microbe or pest.

I tried to imagine Sasha patrolling the airport. All I could conjure up was her accidentally knocking over a toddler in order to pull a Twizzler out of the child's mouth. I got a chance to observe the brigade in action when I was cleared to spend part of an afternoon at Dulles airport following a team. Just past the luggage carousel for international flights, I met Canine Enforcement Officer Jennifer Jones and her dog, Paisley.

We sat and talked in Jennifer's small office, decorated with Snoopy stuffed animals, beagle calendars, and trading cards with pictures of Beagle Brigade dogs and their vital statistics. Paisley, a slender two-year-old with intense, dark-rimmed eyes, rested in her crate. She was a failed pet who was turned in to the pound, and met the requirements of the Beagle Brigade. "We are looking for food drive. High energy. A dog that's healthy and not afraid of anything," Jennifer said.

Paisley was Jennifer's second dog; they'd only been together six months. Her previous dog, Quincy, retired after six years on the job and now lives with Jennifer. It is standard for officers to adopt their dogs. During their working life the dogs are kept in a kennel at night. In order to keep the dogs sharp, they aren't allowed to indulge in the life of a pet. Like many retirees, Quincy was having some difficulty making the transition to a life of leisure. "He's driving me nuts," Jennifer said with a sigh. "When he joined the Beagle Brigade he'd been found on the streets and was in a shelter. I don't think he's ever been in a home. He doesn't know the coffee table isn't a springboard."

A Beagle Brigade officer gets three months of training, and a beagle about two months at the National Detector Dog Training Center in Orlando, Florida, run by the U.S. Department of Agriculture. There the dogs learn to recognize five basic foods we do not want coming into the United States: apple, citrus, mango, beef, and pork. In Orlando, they are trained to sit when they detect the odors, and are rewarded with a food treat. Once they realize what the training is about, "You can almost see the lightbulb go on," said Jennifer.

The dogs are also evaluated for their ability to negotiate the chaos of an airline terminal. "I've had dogs that wouldn't come out of the office," said Jennifer. "Others run and climb on the carousel with their tails wagging, like they've never had more fun."

One theme that emerged from Jennifer's stories is that many people become unhinged over their fruit and sausages. Jennifer once was attacked with an apple. Her dog, Quincy, alerted on the woman's purse, and when Jennifer asked to see what was inside, the woman pulled out an apple, started screaming, and hit Jennifer in the face with it. "She was arrested for assaulting a federal officer," said Jennifer. "She pled guilty and spent five nights in jail, then went home to Norway." A modern version, with beagle instead of serpent, of punishment for having the forbidden fruit.

Quincy once alerted on a woman's suitcase, but the woman assured Jennifer she had none of the verboten food items. Jennifer had the bag put through X-ray and found nothing. But every time she brought Quincy back to the suitcase he sniffed and sat. Finally, after feeling around, Jennifer found the contraband: a couple of pounds of sausage sewn into the lining. "The lady said, 'I don't know how it got there,'" Jennifer recalled with a snort.

Many travelers use that excuse. Once, her dog alerted on an old man's bag; he had mangoes. He claimed it wasn't his fault. "My mother packed this bag," he said. Jennifer demanded another look at his passport. "He was eighty-seven years old!" she said.

It was three P.M. and a flight from Austria was coming in. "Austrian Air tends to have a lot of sausage," Jennifer said as she released Paisley from her crate. We stepped from Jennifer's office into the terminal and I was immediately overwhelmed: the cacophony of languages; the barrage of announcements; carts, wheelchairs, and strollers pushing past; the haggard, lost, exhausted travelers. Paisley bounced along, giving a quick sniff to each bag Jennifer pointed to. Most people ignored them. Occasionally Paisley sniffed the foot of a baby in a stroller. Sometimes a traveler bent down to pat her.

Paisley made a line for a white plastic bag carried by a man waiting for his luggage. She sniffed and sat. Jennifer asked him if he had any fruit and he opened the bag and pulled out a large orange. Jennifer marked his customs declaration form, so the gate officer would confiscate the fruit. As she spoke to the man, Paisley, still seated, stared at Jennifer. You could read her mind. "Jennifer, I found an *orange*. Where's my treat?" When Jennifer finished with the man, she dropped a couple of dog food pellets into Paisley's mouth. Another man, watching the encounter, remarked, "That's the first time I've seen a beagle do anything but hunt for rabbits."

Paisley stopped at a young woman's carry-on. Jennifer asked her to open the bag; inside was an orange and banana. Bananas are banned, too. That reminded Jennifer of the time Quincy jumped up on the backpack of a young man heading toward the exit, and hung on by his front paws. The man was bananas for bananas; he had two bunches in the pack.

After ninety minutes, I was ready to go. I was having flashbacks to too many trips spent looking for lost luggage or waiting for a canceled flight to be rescheduled. As I was leaving, Jennifer pointed out another officer patrolling the area with a black Labrador. They were from another arm of Homeland Security, the Canine Enforcement Program, which has dogs searching for currency, drugs, and explosives.

I was intrigued by the difference between training a beagle to find bratwust and a Labrador to find LSD, so I got permission from the department to visit their Canine Enforcement and Training Center in the Blue Ridge mountains.

The center is situated on 250 bucolic acres. As I sat in the lobby waiting for the head of the Canine Enforcement Program, Lee Titus, to give me a tour, a five-month-old Labrador puppy, Quota, dozed next to me in his crate. Titus, a broad-shouldered man in a blue uniform, has spent his entire law enforcement career wrapped up with dogs. There is a photo of him at age nineteen, when he was with the Air Force security police in Okinawa, kneeling next to a German shepherd guard dog.

There are usually about 120 dogs, mostly Labradors and golden retrievers, in various stages of training at the center. Dogs' duties are strictly segregated; a currency dog is never exposed to drugs or explosives, for example. Law enforcement doesn't want the accused to be able to make the claim the dog was confused by competing odors.

Titus grabbed a big bag of finely shredded dollars, a training aid for currency detector dogs. He said the dogs are taught to respond only to a certain threshold of money, to avoid the disaster of having the dogs alerting to the wallets of every traveler. "When a narcotics dog hits on a suitcase it's narcotics," said Titus. "When an explosive dog hits, you know what you do?" he asked.

I shook my head.

"Run!" he said, showing off a little Homeland Security humor. He said the handlers actually notify explosives experts.

He grabbed a photograph of his late dog, Kahlua, a golden retriever, after she made an alert on a crate with a false bottom that contained $570,000. Kahlua is seated by the money, looking content with a rolled-up white towel in her mouth. "That's her reward," Titus explained. He told about another dog of his, Kirby, who was asked to take a look at a 727 Eastern Airlines jet that had arrived from Cali, Colombia. That daily flight was the bread-and-butter plane for both drug smugglers and narcotics agents. But after a thorough search, the human inspector had turned up nothing. Within minutes, Kirby was in the airplane restroom indicating the slot in the wall for razor disposal. The inspectors unscrewed the panel and pulled out eight bricks of cocaine.

"Officially Kirby got a rolled towel," said Titus. "Unoffically, I gave him two cheeseburgers."

"What's with the towel?" I asked.

"The rolled towel is their paycheck," said Titus. "Their meaning in life is to play with that towel. We find dogs that want to do nothing but play with that towel."

To demonstrate he took me to one of their training buildings. Inside was a mail-sorting belt from a post office. A few minutes after we arrived a dog breeder from South Carolina showed up with an eighteen-month-old German shepherd he hoped to sell to the government for about $3,500. "We're looking to see how bad he wants that towel," said Titus.

We watched as an officer threw a towel up the sorting belt. The dog instantly ran up the metal ramp and captured it. Then the officer took the towel and put it under a heavy metal doormat. The dog wrestled it free. The officer turned on the sorting belt, to see if the noise and movement scared the dog. He tossed the towel on it, and without hesitation, the dog ran up the moving belt and grabbed the towel in his mouth. It all took less than a minute.

"That dog is sold," said Titus.

He showed me a piece of equipment they use to train dogs to detect odors. It looked like a row of bleachers that instead of seats had cans set in holes. Inside the cans the trainers place the substance the dog is being trained to identify, be it heroin or explosives. Hidden underneath the bleacher is an officer, flat on his or her back, on one of those roller carts used to inspect automobile undercarriages. If the dog sits when it detects an odor, the officer hidden under the bleacher is given a signal and shoots a rolled white towel through the hole.

I thought of how wonderful the world would be if people responded this way to a rolled white towel.

Me (to husband at the end of the day): I'm too tired to make dinner, it's your turn.
Husband: Hey, I'm exhausted.
Me (using seductive voice): If you cook tonight, you'll get something you've been wanting for days.
Husband: I thought you were tired.
Me: I'm not too tired to roll up a white towel for you, baby.
Husband: Let me in that kitchen!

My reverie was interrupted when Titus indicated we should move to another building. There he showed me his latest training device, a long wooden box that looked like a coffin for a boa constrictor. Since 9/11 the agency's focus had shifted somewhat from narcotics to explosives. Titus had just come into possession of a surface-to-air missile, the kind of shoulder-fired device that can bring down an airplane. Titus was going to nail the missile into the box, put it in a warehouse piled with other goods, and see if one of his new officer-and-dog teams could identify it. A surface-to-air missile seemed a long way from sausage. It was a reminder of the grim reality of our world.

I asked Titus if he had dogs of his own. "I have a sheltie that sheds like crazy, and a five-year-old black Lab who is the most disobedient dog in the world. He's always running away."

"Can't you train him with a towel?" I asked.

"His attitude is, 'I'm supposed to get that? I don't think so!'"

There was no better mood lifter than a professional dog trainer with a misbehaving dog.

26

A BAGEL WHO'S A LOX

Our latest foster, Goldy.

During the time we had houseguests, Laura, from BREW, would send polite periodic inquiries about when we'd be ready for our next perfect foster dog. Finally, we were, and Laura directed me to take a look on the Web site at Goldy. She appeared to be a bagel—that's what BREW calls a beagle–basset hound mix. She had the long, drooping ears and hangdog look of the basset. Her eyes had some of the famous beagle mascara, but her basset lineage made it look like she'd been crying and the mascara was smeared.

Goldy was found when a pickup truck stopped in front of a driveway, the door opened, and Goldy got tossed out. I was beginning to think that when people bought pickup trucks they should be forced to sign a "Nondiscard of beagle" codicil. The family that lived at the end of the driveway took in poor Goldy to join their three kids, two dogs, and two cats. That couldn't last and she ended up with BREW. The Web site said she was crate-trained and hadn't had any accidents. I assumed that meant she was holding it until she got to my house.

I told my daughter we were getting a dog named Goldy, but that maybe we should call her Golda, because we already had a cat named Goldie. "Mom, Goldie the cat has no idea what his name is, so he won't get confused when you call Goldy the dog." Very true.

Rita, a BREW volunteer, brought Goldy to our door. She was smaller and more compact than in her picture on the Web site. Her fur was matted and greasy and rank, but she had just been spayed so we couldn't give her a bath for the next ten days. She had been through so much that when Sasha came over with her head-bite greeting, Goldy just lay down and curled up in a ball.

This seemed to be her preferred posture to the world. When it came time to let her out, no amount of persuasion could rouse her, so we carried her outside. We also carried her to her food bowl and up to her crate. She was clearly in pain from her recent surgery; she spent most of her conscious time chewing at the incision. It had been closed with staples designed with sharp, outward points in order to discourage licking. The flaw in this theory was that she kept licking anyway, and the metal barbs caused a sore mouth, as well.

For the first two days we carried her outside and she would squat as if to pee, then hunch over and move from place to place, with no urine escaping. I called Laura who said it was not unusual for a scared foster to hold it for an inordinate length of time and that if she'd had a bladder infection she'd be peeing everywhere.

At least she ate. But watching her eat was heartbreaking. After being carried to her food bowl she would nibble a few morsels, then slink to another room, see that all was clear, furtively return to the bowl for a few more bites, then slink away again.

As passive as she normally was, she became Hulk-like when we tried to put her in the crate. I aimed her face toward the opening and shoved, but by the time I huffed past her resistance and got her hind end in, she had turned her head back around to the front and pushed out past me before I could get the door shut. On the occasions I succeeded at locking her up she spent the rest of the night wailing like Lear on the moor. My daughter—in whose room we kept the crates—came stumbling out at two A.M. to say she couldn't sleep.

Moving the crate to another room and shutting the door was no better, we could still hear her moaning and attempts to break out. This is where we fell down as dog owners. If Goldy was going to be someone's permanent dog we should show her that we were the leaders and she would just have to get used to the crate. We needed to accept that she was going to keep us up until she learned that lesson. But we wanted to sleep. So we brought her into our bedroom and taught her to lie down on a towel on the floor.

She seemed content. So content that we had to pick her up in the morning and carry her downstairs in order to take her for a walk. I was starting to get alarmed by day four when I had yet to see any release of urine. In addition, the time she wasn't sleeping, she spent under the dining room table chewing on her incision. I took her to my vet.

Although BREW had estimated Goldy was two to four years old, my vet said, examining her teeth, that she was only eighteen months to two years. But she showed me that Goldy's white teeth had been worn down almost to the gum line. I asked why.

"She probably was in a cage all the time, chewing at the bars," she said.

Aha! No wonder she confused "crate" with "cage." The vet said that her bladder was not distended and there was no sign of infection, so she was secretly urinating somewhere. But her incision was oozing. The vet prescribed antibiotics and painkillers and a collar, one of those lampshade getups that go around their necks and keep them from making contact with the rest of their body. I got Goldy home and put the collar on. She began an awkward dance in which she tried to reach her staples, but only banged the plastic collar on the ground. She looked like she was trying to imitate—very badly—Pixar's anthropomorphic desk lamp mascot.

The collar took her disposition from sadness to misery. We couldn't find a way to relieve her gloom, but she did start relieving herself all over our rugs. As I got back on my hands and knees to apply pet stain remover, I started wondering if perhaps I had come to the end of taking in "housebroken" fosters.

The only time she came to life was when she saw a chance to escape. If she was in our backyard and one of us was going out through the fence she would suddenly be there, trying to push her way into the wide world. One day when I was taking out the garbage she succeeded. I had been carrying this twenty-five-pound slug of a dog up and down the stairs for a week, but now she was running like Marion Jones down the middle of our street, heading for one of the city's main thoroughfares.

As I chased after her, I saw cars swerving around her. At one point she ran up onto the sidewalk a block ahead of me and stopped. A pedestrian was nearby and I screamed, "Can you please grab her collar?" I looked and sounded crazy. The woman might have complied if I'd yelled, "I want your wallet!" But as for grabbing a strange dog's collar, she just shook her head. As I got within reach of Goldy she regathered her strength and shot back into the middle of the road. Finally, as she approached the intersection where certain death awaited, she lay down panting.

I scooped her up and carried her the three blocks home. "Hey, couch potato, do you know how close you were to becoming mashed potato?" I asked her. "I'm not going to buy your 'I'm too depressed to get up' act anymore."

It was time for me to write Goldy's entry on the BREW Web site. Where to begin? "She'll scream all night and pee on your rug all day." "As you carry her inside and out, upstairs and down, you will enjoy your upper body workout." "You won't even notice she's there until she runs outside and gets hit by a car."

In the end I mentioned her worn-down teeth and her gentle, stoic nature. It was not a strong sell. Only one person called. She was pregnant (naturally!) with her third child. I had doubts that Goldy would be right for such a family at all. Then the woman mentioned that they were taking care of a friend's golden retriever, but she was very disturbed that when the dog drank from its bowl some water spilled onto the kitchen floor. I marveled that a mother of two children under five would even notice such a thing, but by the end of the conversation—against my own interest—I told her Goldy would not be a good fit.

As the days dragged on and no one contacted us about Goldy, my husband started lobbying for her return to BREW. "She's a sweet dog and I feel sorry for her, but she's a big lump who's ruining the carpets." I didn't disagree, but I thought things would change once her collar came off and her staples came out. When the blessed day came I put her in the tub and washed out months— possibly a lifetime—of grime. But afterward she went back to her favorite spot under the dining room table and refused Sasha's invitation to play. She did discover our shoes, however. "She's got to go," my husband said, when I warned him to put his shoes away after I barely rescued his favorite pair of slip-ons.

Goldy found she could leap from the floor of our bedroom to our bed, and once she did there was no persuading her to stay on the towel. The problem was that while the dogs were blissful on the bed together, my husband and I didn't have enough room to turn over. I started to feel as though I was running the world's most eccentric boardinghouse, where all the guests insisted on sleeping with us and peeing on our floor. At least they didn't demand I cook them a hot meal.

We started calling Goldy Uncle Harry, because she was truly phlegmatic, repeatedly and explosively clearing her throat. She also was allergic to something—possibly cats—because she kept making a sound as if she had a Ping-Pong ball caught in her throat. She had done it a couple of times with the vet who explained it was a "reverse sneeze." How about developing "reverse pee," I thought to myself. At night she snored so forcefully that the vibrations reminded me of having a purring cat on the bed. Because of our inability to sleep with both dogs on the bed we started to put Sasha in her crate at night. It didn't seem right, however, that our permanent dog was being pushed out this way. "This isn't fair, we're crating Sasha so this lug can sleep on the bed," my husband said. "Call BREW."

I sent an e-mail to Laura saying that we weren't sure how long we could keep Goldy. She asked if we could take her to their upcoming adoption event. That was the solution! I'd seen Laura in action, convincing people they couldn't live without whatever insecure, unhousebroken beagle was underfoot—she'd sold me one. In a few more days, we'd find Goldy a new home.

27

WILSON, LADYBUG, AND PUGSLEY

Amazing stories of survival.

The following Saturday morning husband, daughter, and I drove an hour and a half to a pet emporium for a beagle giveaway.

The first problem was that simultaneous with BREW's adoption event was one for retired racing greyhounds. These magnificent animals were gathered at the door, tall and lean with fine, velvety fur. No wonder the pharaohs revered protogreyhounds. I kept finding myself drawn to these creatures, so self-contained and noble.

There were a dozen or so beagles milling in the next aisle. I immediately noticed that almost every person milling near them had a BREW ID tag. Where were all the adopters, where was Goldy's new family? I found Laura, who sighed and said it had been really slow so far. The three of us wandered around with Goldy, scanning the faces for fresh beagle-seekers. There were none, but we were immediately drawn to a little beagle mix. He was being held by a woman in her seventies. The dog wasn't up for adoption, she explained, he was the family pet. She was watching him while her granddaughter tried to pitch her foster beagle to the empty room.

The woman said the dog was a beagle–Jack Russell mix. He had the excitable terrier personality, jumping up on us for pats and wagging his almost tailless rump. I asked if he was born without a tail.

"No, they cropped it," she said. "I hate that. To my mind it's a mutilation. Why would you mutilate the back end of a dog? It should be outlawed! The only thing worse I can think of is circumcision!"

My husband's eyebrows shot up. "Oy vey," he mumbled.

We continued wandering. A BREW volunteer saw my name tag and came over and introduced herself. Her name was Teresa and it turned out she had fostered Goldy after Goldy had been passed on from the family that found her.

Teresa gave Goldy a hug and said she had been such a wonderful foster that she was moved from outdoor dog status to indoor, one of only two current fosters to merit that promotion.

"How many dogs do you have?" I asked.

"Ten of my own—they're mostly seniors now, they live in the house. I have twenty-one fosters outside."

I didn't say anything, but I felt my eyebrows involuntarily shoot up.

"Yes. I'm nuts," she said. She wasn't the first dog activist I'd met who described herself that way because of a nutty number of dogs. Yet these people clearly weren't nuts. It was too bad that they had to reflexively explain away their life's passion as a mental aberration.

Her outdoor dogs were all beagles; in her backyard kennels she housed most of the dogs on the BREW Web site. Like many fanatic dog people I met, her passion was stoked by a need to rectify childhood wrongs. When she was a girl Teresa's father raised beagles in rural Virginia. Down there, she explained, they aren't considered pets. They're hunting dogs and you get them for $25 or less. The owners had about as much attachment to the dogs as to a pair of gym socks. And like gym socks, when beagles got worn out, they got tossed out.

Teresa said her indoor dogs were a variety of breeds: rat terrier, miniature dachshund, blue tick coonhound, various mutts. "My ten are all rejects." She said at mealtime she lines up their bowls and they all wait patiently because they know the order they're being fed. Goldy, when she was living there, was temporarily number one. Teresa said Goldy had whiled away her time by sleeping and snoring on the couch. Her previous foster had made a special note that Goldy had "loved" being in her crate. And while she was at Teresa's she was perfectly housebroken. I was getting sick of this—taking in dogs who were housebroken before they met me and housebroken afterward. Maybe dogs, in addition to hearing sounds humans couldn't, could see things humans couldn't—such as the only-visible-to-dogs sign hanging over our front door that said, WELCOME TO THE PEE PARTY.

I asked Teresa how she started in the dog rescue business (in part so I could monitor any similar symptoms in myself). She told me about one of her first dogs, Ladybug. It was a bitterly cold winter and Teresa's father-in-law was driving on an access road south of Charlottesville when he saw a tiny, white Chihuahua chewing on a deer carcass. It was an amazing primal scene: a fist-sized dog with the heart of a lion. One could almost imagine the Chihuahua, an abandoned or lost pet, a refugee from Mexico, finding itself in frozen, rural Virginia and realizing that in order to live, it had to take down a deer.

As soon as Teresa's father-in-law got home he called and told her about the dog. She was stricken—but unlike most of us, who would say, "Oh, how terrible," and promptly forget about it,

Teresa immediately got in her car. She found the deer-gnawing Chihuahua, but when she got out of her car to rescue it, it ran across the interstate. By then it was dark and Teresa was not able to give chase. At this point, most dog lovers would shrug and say, "I've done what I could." But Teresa started driving by the area daily, searching for the piece of fluff. Eventually, she found her; the dog was chasing mice in a farmer's field. Again she tried to catch the dog, but it was too wily. So she talked to the farmer who agreed to let her set out a humane trap for the dog. You don't get to be the Daniel Boone of Chihuahuas by falling for the humane-trap ploy, and the dog remained free.

Then one Saturday the farmer called: The dog was in the barn. Teresa quickly rounded up a posse and they all went to the farm. As soon as Teresa and her friends arrived at the barn door, the dog shot out. But now it was only feet from the trap. They surrounded the dog to force it into the trap. Although the dog had obviously been injured and could not run very fast, it managed to elude them by diving into a groundhog hole filled with ice water. Teresa put her hand in and the dog bit it. A friend produced a pair of sturdy gloves, they pulled the bedraggled creature out, put it in a carrying case, and drove it to the veterinarian.

The dog had to be muzzled for the examination. She was missing a toe, and her hip had been broken as well as her ribs. The dog had probably been thrown from a car and had lain by the side of the road until the fractures healed. She weighed six pounds. Teresa took her home in the case and while she was cooking dinner told her husband not to touch the dog. When Teresa came back into the room her husband was stroking her. They named her Ladybug and she was a loving pet for eight years.

One of her more recent acquisitions was the coonhound, Wilson, that Teresa's nephew had adopted from the pound for the purpose of raccoon hunting. Coonhounds have the same social status in rural Virginia as beagles. The fact that Wilson had been in the pound—think of it as hunting-dog rehab—didn't bode well for his prowess. Teresa was keeping the dog temporarily when she noticed that every time he tried to urinate he would hunch over in pain.

She took him to the vet and discovered why his hunting days had come to an abrupt end. He had been shot in the penis. The pellet was still lodged there. She paid to have the pellet removed and his urethra rerouted through what was left of his organ. But when the rerouting healed so much scar tissue formed that again he was unable to urinate. She took him back to the vet where he was neutered and his urethra given a different detour, this time through the place where his scrotum had been.

Teresa was becoming more and more attached to the dog. Despite—or perhaps because of—these assaults to his manhood, he was a calm and devoted soul. Now Teresa was stuck with the bill for his new underpass, which the doctor knocked down to $300 from $600. Teresa went on the Internet and put out a plea through the county shelter's Web site for donations for Wilson's genital gyrations. She wasn't expecting much, but shortly afterward a check from Washington, D.C., arrived for the entire amount. Maybe it was from a lobbyist for a urological society.

Now that Wilson was healed, sending him back out on the raccoon-hunting circuit seemed sure to provoke hideous memories. Teresa felt she couldn't keep him, but she had gotten him house-trained and crate-trained, so she found a family to adopt him. A day later Teresa got a frantic phone call. Wilson had destroyed the blinds and eaten the rug. "Take him back!" She picked him up immediately and when she let him out in her driveway he ran around joyously. "That was three years ago and I've never had a minute's trouble with him," she said.

When Teresa told me about her first beagle, I understood why she had developed such an attachment to the breed. Teresa's sister's boyfriend had beagles as hunting dogs. One of them was an older female. Despite dogs' close association with humans they have yet to adopt some of our finer biological innovations, such as the missionary position (they must call it "human style") and menopause. The lack of menopause is a decided miscalculation. Imagine it in human terms—you could be bringing a cake to the nursing home to celebrate Grandma's ninetieth birthday, only to be told she's in labor and delivery.

This elderly female hunting dog was pregnant. One day, as Teresa's sister was at the kitchen sink doing dishes, she saw the dog in the backyard. The dog had created a hole with her paws and now she was filling it back up. Then the sister realized why the dog was doing this—she was burying her litter. Teresa's sister ran to rescue the pups. She herself pawed at the dirt and uncovered six little ones, five of them dead. She picked up the lone survivor, took him into the house, and called Teresa, who said she would be right over to pick up the benighted creature.

Teresa got formula and a tiny bottle, but the dog, now named Pugsley, wouldn't suckle. (I found out why in Raymond Coppinger's book. A newborn pup must suckle almost immediately or forever lose that ability. Humans too must learn shortly after birth, or have to be mechanically fed until they can swallow food at around six months.) Teresa trimmed the fingernail on her pinky, dipped it in formula and put it into the puppy's mouth. She slept on the couch and every few hours woke and finger-fed him. He survived.

Not surprisingly, he grew up with an inflated sense of self and liked to boss Teresa around. But he was feisty and charming and she loved him. When Pugsley was eighteen months old he failed to come home one day. Teresa spent the next twenty-four hours searching for him. She found him bloody and bashed in a ditch.

He had been hit by a car, and three disks in his back were compressed. The local vet was of the old-fashioned patch-em-up or put-em-down school of medicine. He told Teresa just to let the dog heal and he might be all right. He wasn't. He lost feeling in and most of the use of his back legs.

Teresa cut a pant leg, put a slit in it, and put Pugsley's back end through it, so she could hold him up while he walked on his front legs. Teresa took Pugsley swimming every day to build up his strength. Pugsley had the spirit of a hunting dog and still wanted to run in the country and chase small creatures. Teresa's husband built a cart with wheels that they would attach him to with a harness. Teresa's father was driven crazy by the fact that not only did his daughter have a beagle for a pet, but it was a beagle that looked as if he could star in a canine version of *Porgy and Bess*.

Pugsley lived for nine more years. Teresa spent a good portion of those years searching the woods for Pugsley's cart. He would go out and get so excited chasing something that he would become detached from his cart and end up dragging himself home. "He had so much personality," she said, tearing up. "I loved him so much."

Just at that emotional moment, Laura came over to tell me that a single mother with two small children had expressed an interest in Goldy. I ran to find her.

28

FOOL'S GOLDY

Won't someone adopt this dog?

Laura described the woman who wanted to meet Goldy, but I couldn't find her anywhere in the BREW crowd. Goldy and I started making a larger circuit around the store and finally I saw her next to a greyhound with a brindle coat. She was staring at it transfixed and rhythmically stroking its fur.

"I hear you're looking for Goldy," I said, indicating Goldy.

"Oh," she said, snapping out of her spell as she looked at the squat, fat, wrinkle-faced dog at my feet. She turned back to the brindle and began stroking again. "These dogs are so beautiful," she murmured. "I thought they would be a lot of trouble, but they say they're very quiet and gentle dogs."

"So, Goldy is really sweet," I said, like Cinderella's stepmother trying to palm off her ugly daughter. Goldy, seeming to understand the stakes, looked up at the woman and nudged her leg. She leaned down and patted Goldy's coarse hair.

"So, what got you interested in beagles?" I continued, trying to use a subtle brainwashing technique.

"Beagles are smaller than I expected," she said, still peering at Goldy. "I think I want more of a dog." She stood, turned back to the greyhound and resumed stroking the handsome prince. Goldy and I wandered back to Laura.

"How'd it go?" Laura asked.

"Greyhounds are better-looking than beagles," I said.

So it went for the rest of the afternoon. Every time I dragged Goldy up to someone with a searching look on his or her face it turned out to be another BREW volunteer looking for adopters. Toward the end I got in a conversation with Laura and some other BREW people about hard-to-place dogs.

"Well, we thought Sasha might come back," Laura said. "She seemed like a mess and we didn't know anything about her." Everyone laughed at how they took bets about how long it would be before we called in defeat.

Let them laugh. I felt a surging pride in my family and Sasha. We had inadvertently picked her for her stunted personality. Yet in our stumbling we had unlocked the wonderful dog inside her.

My husband walked up and said we should go. Laura held out her hand and said, "Okay, let me have Goldy."

"Why?" I said. "She hasn't been placed."

"I thought you said you couldn't take it anymore," she said.

My husband's face lit up. "That's right. We can't. Bye, Goldy. Let's go."

I had convinced myself that once Goldy's staples came out her real personality would emerge. I decided her problem had been that lying on the floor chewing on staples for twenty-two hours a day left no time for self-expression. It turned out lying on the floor twenty-two hours a day, minus chewing on staples, was her personality. She was a bummer of a dog, but I just couldn't hand her back. What if they sent her to a vet's office where she'd have to stay in a crate all day? Her hideous wailing began to echo in my head. Anyway, after the infection, the collar, the carrying, the hand-feeding, the rug-deodorizing, I couldn't just admit defeat like this.

"Oh, she's coming around. We'll take her back with us."

"Coming around? She acts like she's barely come to," said my husband. "Hand over the leash."

Laura looked at us, her expression saying, "Just make a decision about the dog; I don't want to know this much about your marriage." My husband was right, of course. Taking back Goldy meant being stuck with Goldy, because who is looking for an unaffectionate, unhousebroken dog? But I held on to the leash and my husband just shrugged.

The BREW people took sympathy on me. Rita, who had delivered Goldy to our house, took a series of new pictures of her for the Web site. She had her pose next to a basketball to show Goldy, though hefty, was actually petite. Rita even said she would make Goldy "Featured Beagle of the Week," which I now realized was BREW-speak for "Merchandise we can't move."

In the car Goldy lay slothlike on my daughter's leg ("Mom, she's squishing my thigh!"). Why did I do it? It was not so much to show my devotion to a dog, but to show my connection to dog people. I wanted the BREW people to think I was one of them. I was trying to prove that I was not just a dog person— what's so special about someone who loves her dog?—I was one of those devote-my-life-to-discarded-dogs dog people. This was even beyond my mother or sister, who only went gaga over their own dogs.

Before I starting hammering together a kennel for twenty-one beagles, we resumed life with Goldy. It was not good. I did my best to write up a new description to go with her new picture and prominent position on the Web site.

"Goldy has made great progress on the house-training front.

She really likes her walks, but she equally likes her naps. She would be a good companion for an individual or family that is away a lot during the day (just give her a comfy place to snooze). She is so sweet and undemanding." The silence that followed made it clear even the most naïve person could translate this into: "She's a slug on a rug—a wet rug."

And so it went. Goldy spent her days under the dining room table. Despite my frequent outings with her, I would often find her hauling herself into the den to relieve her bladder.

The den was becoming a wasteland, the carpet so full of urine, enzyme sprays, pet-stain removers, deodorizers, spilled juice, and tears that it felt like quicksand. A miasma formed over the rug, and I worried that it was endangering my daughter's health. I wasn't going to invest in professional carpet cleaning again until we had Goldy out of the picture. I repeatedly sprayed the carpet with the enzyme gloop.

The enzymes were supposed to consider the bacteria from the animal waste in the carpet the equivalent of the five-star meal. Once they finished feasting, the smell would be gone. But what happened in my rug was like the lobsters at a lobster shack rising up and snapping the patrons to death. My bacteria were clearly more powerful than their enzymes. Next, I sprinkled baking soda over the rug, but instead of absorbing the smell, it left highlights of every urination, like chalk outlines of bodies.

One morning, about a half hour before we were to have a houseful of people over for brunch, my husband walked into the den and declared, "This room reeks. We can't have guests."

"Well, I've got a casserole in the oven and they're on their way. Should we just not answer the doorbell when they arrive?"

"We absolutely have to do something. This is disgusting," he said. "I know. Make a pot of mulled cider. That always makes the house smell great."

"It's *July*!" I said. "Do you want us to put on earmuffs, hand people the cider, and sing 'Wassail'?"

I searched in a cabinet and found some probably toxic powder that promised it was a miracle deodorizer. It did work well enough that it held the scent down for the duration of the brunch without visibly sickening any of our friends. I thought I had fooled everyone until a guest called to thank me, and said when she and her husband and son got into the car they all burst out laughing about our animal situation. "We kept saying, 'How do they live like that?'" she told me, laughing again.

We were running out of hope when I got an e-mail from BREW asking if I would check out the home of a potential adopter. It was a young couple looking for a low-maintenance beagle. Mary Lou, the BREW representative, suggested I bring Goldy and give her a hard sell. My daughter, Goldy, and I drove to the apartment in Dupont Circle. "Please, Goldy, whatever you do, don't go in their house," I said as we rang the bell.

The apartment was tiny, but since it was bigger than a crate, I felt it was just right for Goldy. Although I was supposed to be interviewing them, I kept pointing out how Goldy was the perfect apartment dog. "She's very nice," said the woman. "But we really hope we get Molly," she said, referring to another lazy beagle on the BREW Web site. I felt like saying, "I've got the power here and it's Goldy or nothing." However, I approved them and the following week they adopted Molly. Goldy went back under the dining room table.

Then Sunday night rolled around. My husband and I were deep into a season-long cop series on HBO. We had had dinner, put our daughter to bed, cleaned the kitchen, scooped the litter box, and were settling down on the couch when I went to look for the remote. I found it next to Goldy. Despite her worn-down teeth, she had managed to chew through the innards of it.

I took it to the den and tried clicking. Nothing.

"She ate the remote!" bellowed my husband. "That's it! Go upstairs, write an e-mail to BREW, and get rid of her."

"We can still change the channel. We just have to get up and do it manually," I said, standing in front of the TV. I realized this was like saying, "We can also knit our own socks and thresh our own wheat."

"Send the e-mail!" he said, as he got up off the couch and furiously pressed the buttons on the TV.

I sent it.

The next day Laura called and said Rita's husband, Kent, would come and get Goldy. Laura kept reassuring me that it wasn't my fault and I shouldn't feel guilty, but I thought that now she'd never be adopted. Kent came the next day and explained that he and Rita would keep Goldy until they found a new family for her. They already had five dogs of their own and six foster dogs, so they would barely notice her. I said good-bye and he walked Goldy to the van. She sat in the front seat and put her paws on the dashboard so she could see the road ahead. As soon as they turned the corner, I set out for Radio Shack and bought a new remote.

Two weeks later Rita sent me an e-mail saying Goldy had a new home. It was my description of her worn-down teeth that had attracted the family, two women who only took in difficult cases. They had previously adopted four BREW beagles, but two had died recently; their only worry about Goldy was that she wasn't hard-core enough. Fortunately, when Rita brought her to their house, Goldy promptly pooped on their oriental carpet. That sealed the deal.

After Roscoe, Maggie, Annie, and Goldy, it seemed so quiet now with just our three permanent animals, as if the world's longest sleepover party had just come to an end. All during the foster period we had been taking Sasha, along with whatever new dog was in residence, for more training with Todd. The first time we all showed up with Sasha and Roscoe, Todd asked what was going on. I told him I'd gotten an emergency e-mail from our rescue organization.

"This came from an e-mail?" he said to my husband, indicating Roscoe.

"Yes. It was her idea," my husband said, indicating me.

"I've got a way to fix that. Take a big glass of water and pour it over your computer," Todd said. I didn't know what to make of the fact that a man who made his living from dogs now thought I was an over-the-edge dog nut.

29

DOMESTICATED
TRANQUILITY

Where did dogs come from?

While I was pregnant, I obsessively read pregnancy books. This was surely counterproductive. Because of the anxiety I experienced over that glass of wine I had before I knew I was pregnant, or whether wearing rubber gloves and a surgical mask was protecting my fetus from litter-box-contracted toxoplasmosis, I surely ended up bathing her in more stress hormones than if I'd remained ignorant. Once I had my daughter, I was too overwhelmed taking care of her to read the stack of books on the nightstand about how I should be taking care of her.

With Sasha I decided to combine the ignorant and overwhelmed approach. My dog reference books consisted of a tear-streaked and dog-eared copy of *Housebreaking and Training Your New Puppy* and the too-well-illustrated *Dog Owner's Home Veterinary Handbook* (I advise skipping the photos of demodectic mange, and oral papillomatosis, also known as "warts in the mouth").

Now that Sasha had settled down into being lovable and exasperating, I wanted to find out more about the dog who would be spending the next twelve years with us, and about the dogs who had been spending the past twelve millennia with us. Besides reading Coppinger's book, I picked up two by James Serpell, director of the Center for the Interaction of Animals and Society at the University of Pennsylvania School of Veterinary Medicine. One was *In the Company of Animals: A Study of Human-Animal Relationships,* the other the comprehensive-sounding *The Domestic Dog: Its Evolution, Behaviour, and Interactions with People,* a compendium of scientific papers edited by Serpell.

With each paragraph I began to see Sasha not just as a good companion who happened to eat my cell phone charger, but a symbol of the greatest transformation in human experience. Serpell wrote that dogs were the first animals domesticated by humans, far predating the more utilitarian cow or chicken. It is easy to see how dogs, with another set of eyes, and particularly nose, could be useful to hunter-gatherers, but Serpell was not entirely convinced that helpfulness was what led man to tame the wolf, thus begetting the dog. He wrote that the pleasure modern humans experience having dogs as pets may have been the impulse that drove our prehistoric ancestors to bring wolf pups into their huts. Breed the tamest ones to each other, and eventually you get a dog.

To show that affection has always characterized the human-dog relationship, Serpell cited the archeological find in Israel of an approximately twelve-thousand-year old burial site. It contained the bones of an elderly human arranged so that the left hand rested on the shoulder of a five-month-old puppy, "a timeless and eloquent gesture of attachment," Serpell wrote.

Domesticating dogs turned out to be so much fun that humankind went on a domestication binge (you could say humans went whole hog—transforming the wild boar into the pig) and launched the agricultural revolution, which led to modern civilization. I thought of a random list of things that wouldn't exist without modern civilization: brassieres, computer discs, felt-tipped pens. It was no coincidence Sasha had eaten all of these. It was her way of acknowledging that without the dog, we'd still be hunter-gatherers out chasing rabbits. (I doubted I'd do a better job of it than Sasha.)

While Serpell agreed with Charles Darwin that humans created dogs, not everyone does. Coppinger argues that dogs domesticated themselves, and that it happened in a relatively short period of time. His scenario is that when humans started forming relatively stable settlements twelve to fifteen thousand years ago, they left all sorts of delicious waste products around. Although wolves instinctively avoid humans—and would be exceedingly dangerous and difficult for people to raise—a few genetically tamer individuals started hanging around looking for discarded bones. These human-tolerant wolves bred with each other, and voilà, the dog.

Coppinger cites an amazing Russian experiment to back up the theory. From 1959 until his death in 1985, geneticist Dmitri Belyaev bred wild silver foxes. His basic idea was to test each fox's response to humans and then breed the naturally "tamest" of these wild animals to each other. After only six generations, a few of the offspring not only tolerated humans, they desired them. Along with this transformation in behavior came other changes within a few more generations: spotted coats and floppy ears. The foxes were becoming doglike!

Of course, no experiment can answer the ultimate question of whether wolves orchestrated their own domestication, or the earliest human pet lovers did (or if it was some combination of both).

Serpell's books are filled with astounding morsels of information. Dogs were revered in ancient Greece as part of the cult of Asklepios, the god of medicine. At what Serpell calls an ancient health resort, "the dogs that lived around the shrine were specially

trained to lick people . . . since it was believed that these animals
. . . had the power to cure illness with their tongues." I don't
know why it ever stopped. I'd sign up for the package of shiatsu
massage and shih tzu lick anytime.

I also read that Polynesians often suckled puppies. This made
me wonder if the people who object to women breast-feeding
their babies in public would be more, or less, upset to see women
breast-feeding their puppies in public. I later found out this is not
a geographically isolated practice. A Norwegian newspaper
reported about the recent case of a new mother who nursed both
her infant son and a litter of puppies, after her pet dog died giving
birth. The mother, perhaps tacitly acknowledging that Scandinavia
is a long way from the South Seas, was quoted as saying, "I can
accept that some think what I did was nauseating."

Australian Aborigines too have an intensely close relationship
with their dingoes, Serpell wrote. The dogs sleep in the hut, are
given meat and fruit, and are frequently kissed on the snout.
While they are taken as helpers on hunting expeditions, the dingoes often become fatigued, and when they refuse to go on are
slung over the hunters' shoulders and carried home. Also, the
Aborigines eat their fleas. This sounded remarkably like Sasha's
cosseted life. I hated to admit it, but I had the feeling if all flea
medication were suddenly banned, I would be eating Sasha's personal parasites, once I checked their carbohydrate count.

The scientists who wrote *The Domestic Dog* often seemed to
be directly addressing Sasha. Coprophagia, or "eating faeces" was
"more common than expected among animals found unowned
or rescued off the streets." Why should this be unexpected? In
some ways it could be seen as a sign of intrepidness: "Hey baby,
you wouldn't believe the things I developed a taste for during my
roaming years."

I also found the reason for Sasha's desire to tip over the garbage can and consume its contents. When a wolf pack brings down its prey, they want to eat as much as possible as quickly as possible. Who knows where the next meal is coming from? Those with dainty manners will be left gnawing on gristle. The wolf digestive tract is built to handle such supersizing, which is a good thing, because in the forest it's hard to find a veterinarian to do emergency surgery to remove a moose hoof. This desire to gorge, the book explained, particularly remains in the pack hounds, "such as beagles and foxhounds."

I didn't need to read a book to know that compared to the dog, the human sense of smell stinks. But I didn't realize that the beagle's nose should be an object of awe: "An appreciation of the importance of olfaction for the dog can be gained by comparison of the quantity of olfactory epithelium; about 75 cm^2, in the beagle compared to 3 cm^2 in man." Or, in Dave Barry's memorable phrase, beagles are "noses with feet." This epithelial superiority allows dogs to detect concentrations of substances at a level 100 million times lower than humans can.

So exquisite is dogs' sense of smell, I read later in some articles, that British researchers are training dogs to smell out bladder cancer cells in human urine samples. The researchers were inspired by reports that some dogs went crazy sniffing particular moles on their owners, moles that turned out to be cancerous. One dog, as reported in the medical journal the *Lancet*, even tried to bite off an offending mole. This prompted the woman to go to the doctor, who discovered the dog had been trying to remove a melanoma. We probably aren't far from the day when medically trained dogs form a group practice, then refuse to accept their owners' insurance.

All this prompted a revelation as to why dogs have built no civilizations, written no poetry, made no medical discoveries, and why humans have. It's not because of our larger brains, or our opposable thumbs, or our capacity for language. It's because we're not being driven insane all day long by smells. I remembered what it was like in the first months of pregnancy when I developed a doglike ability to detect scents. My husband came home from work, I'd give him a kiss and say, "I begged you not to eat broccoli for lunch or use that salad dressing I hate. That salad dressing is filled with powdered garlic and oregano!"

I could detect scents with bloodhoundlike precision and it drove me crazy. Experiencing smells this way left me unable to think, only sniff. With dog-level epithelium, I would have been able to smell that peanut butter and jelly sandwich my husband ate for lunch the first day of kindergarten.

When I finished Serpell's books, I needed to know more. So I arranged to interview him at his office at the veterinary school. Serpell had on the academic's uniform of sweater, corduroy pants, and glasses. He had a calm, assured manner and a British accent, which gave his every statement an oracular quality.

Serpell wrote at length of the intensity of the connection humans and dogs feel for one another: "The dog-human relationship is arguably the closest we humans can ever get to establishing a dialogue with another sentient life-form . . ." So I started by asking him what kind of dog, or dogs, he had.

"I don't have a dog," he replied.

This was like interviewing Dr. Ruth Westheimer and having her tell me she was a virgin.

"You don't have a dog?" I sputtered.

He explained that since he lived in the city, he thought it was cruel to keep a dog confined. He cited the difficulties his own research assistant was having with her shiba inu. "As soon as she turns her back the dog trashes the house," he said. "She's destroyed thousands of dollars' worth of furniture." At least his research assistant worked at a place with a staff of dog analysts. The shiba inu was going for a consultation at the hospital's behavior clinic later that morning. As always, I was gratified to see that even dog professionals have dog trouble.

Although Serpell had been studying dogs since 1979, he hadn't had one since he was a child. He and his wife and two children had a cat, but the children—ages ten and six—had been lobbying hard for a dog. "I may yet succumb," he said.

"I know what you mean," I said. "That's how I ended up with a beagle. Would you get a beagle?"

"No," he said, giving me a small smile of the sort you give to someone who has just told you, "At night space aliens come in my bedroom and anally probe me."

I ask him why he wouldn't get a beagle—as if I didn't know.

"They're hounds," he said. "Hounds are tricky. They're bred to hunt in packs. They're very nose oriented. They get on a scent trail and they're very difficult to distract. That's what they were wanted for. They're difficult to train. They have a tendency toward obesity—" He stopped, perhaps seeing that he was plunging me into a state of gloom.

"Within any breed you find many individuals who are delightful," he quickly added.

Since he'd brought up hound noses, I offered my newly developed theory about intelligence and the sense of smell. After I laid it out—including the example of smelling my husband's luncheon salad dressing—he gave a small smile identical to the one he'd given when I asked if he'd get a beagle.

I pressed him to tell what kind of dog he'd get if, like me, he'd rather deal with a dog than with his family's nagging.

"Part of me says a shelter dog, part of me says, Oh, my God, don't do that," he said. "I'd give it serious thought. In the end I'd do something random and face the consequences."

I asked him about the drawbacks to shelter dogs—as if I didn't know.

"Not all dogs found in the shelter are bad dogs. But you have a high probability they're in there for a reason: The owner found it hard to live with. Behavior problems are the number one reason people get rid of dogs. But almost no one breeds dogs for good behavior."

He said there are two poles in the dog community. One is the breed clubs. They are obsessed with pure bloodline and appearance. They often disregard temperament and the disease or disability that results from inbreeding. The other is the rescue community, which to prevent the unchecked reproduction of unwanted mutts wants virtually all dogs sterilized. It's an understandable position, but one that prevents what might be the best pets from reproducing. I suddenly had a pang about our first foster beagle, Roscoe. He had already been neutered when we got him, but there should be a million Roscoes.

Serpell had a radical notion to get humans out of the dilemma we have created. "I would love to see a movement to forget about dogs' appearance. Forget it!" he said. "Produce dogs with very good temperaments, dogs that will be great pets. Family pets are what ninety percent of dogs are for."

He and Coppinger agreed on that. Coppinger explained that when we look at a mutt we see a corruption of a purebred dog. But in reality, purebred dogs are corruptions of mutts. He hypothesizes that the first dogs, what he calls "village dogs," looked similar to the kinds of mongrels that fill animal shelters today. They're about thirty pounds with a short, smooth coat, variable coloring, and pointed ears that flop a little at the tip. From that original model, humans—most intensively since the late nineteenth century with the advent of kennel clubs—have created the hundreds of breeds recognized today. Coppinger says mutts are much more likely to be genetically healthy than purebreds.

Serpell and Coppinger also agree that the cosseted life of today's pet dogs can be grotesque. We take working breeds—created to perform a specific function—then freeze their physical characteristics like something out of *The Picture of Dorian Gray*. In the meantime we ignore that their genetics are decaying, causing everything from obsessive compulsive disorders (they want to herd sheep, but are stuck in the living room) to hip dysplasia (the result of limiting breeding stock).

Serpell suggested that under his regime the only nod to appearance would be that dogs bred for good temperament come in small, medium, and large. I could imagine him presenting this concept in a manifesto at the Westminster Dog Show. It would go over about as well as saying to the characters on *Sex and the City*, "Forget those designer high heels. They cost too much money and will eventually give you hammertoe. Shoes are going to be flats and come in small, medium, and large."

Since I wear flats, I liked Serpell's idea. I told him about Roscoe, whose appearance was troubling, but whose personality was a dream. "You're right," I said. "He was the greatest dog, but he can't pass on his genes because having him neutered is part of the adoption agreement."

"Clone him," Serpell suggested.

Our time was up. I wished him luck if his family wore down his resistance to a dog, and told him not to reject the idea of beagles—Roscoe was one, sort of. He gave me that small smile.

30

REACTIVE, GRUMPY, AND DEFENSIVE

Therapy for a mad bulldog.

Since I had come to one of the premier veterinary institutions in the country, I wanted to see what the latest in dog care was. The school's director of communications, Helma Weeks, kindly agreed to give me a tour. The hospital had 28,000 patient visits annually, 11,000 of those coming in through the emergency room. As we walked the corridors, young student doctors with white coats and stethoscopes huddled with older doctors as they looked over patient charts. We passed rooms labeled "Dentistry," "Dermatology," "Cardiology." In every way it had the look and feel of a regular hospital, then I heard a click-click-click and around the corner appeared a patient: a giant schnauzer.

We stopped and watched an operation in progress. A veterinarian and a human surgeon were inserting a liver shunt into a Doberman. I sat with some students behind the huge window looking into the operating room. I was told the procedure we were watching cost $2,000. That was a pittance, I came to realize. One student told me that she'd heard the biggest bill was $40,000.

A spaniel came into the hospital who had been mauled by its canine companion. The spaniel needed everything from transfusions, to repair of internal organs, to skin grafts, to reconstruction of his shredded ears. It took four months to get him to the point where he could walk out of the hospital and return home. He came back through the emergency room a few days later. The other dog had attacked him again.

"Did he make it?" I asked, appalled.

"I don't know," the student said. "But I know everyone here was really mad."

Helma and I continued our tour. We stopped to see kidney dialysis, using a pediatric dialysis unit, being done on an Australian shepherd. We went into the "special species" room. Disconcertingly, when we walked in one of the patients, a parrot, greeted us with a cheerful "Hello!" The parrot was there because she had stopped eating. There was also a chinchilla with heart disease, and a rabbit facing jaw surgery. When we left the parrot called, "Good-bye!"

Helma showed me where the surgeons performed kidney transplants on cats, at a cost of $7,000. That brought to mind the popular urban myth: You go on vacation in some exotic country, have too much to drink at a dark bar, and the next thing you know, you're waking up in a hut and there's a large incision where a kidney used to be. Something like this actually happens to cats! In order to do the kidney transplant, a kidney donor is needed. Since cats aren't known for their humanitarian impulses and don't volunteer their organs, the hospital takes kidneys out of cats used in medical experiments or from shelters. It's actually not a bad deal. The people who are willing to pay for a kidney transplant for their existing cat have to agree to also adopt the donor.

Finally, I was allowed to sit in on a session at the hospital's behavior clinic—although I had missed Dr. Serpell's research assistant's misbehaving shiba inu. At the two-hour $275 session a troubled dog or cat is analyzed by a veterinarian, a nurse-practitioner, and a bunch of veterinary students. I talked to the nurse-practioner, Jenny O'Connor, before the patient arrived: an aggressive French bulldog named Quentin.

Jenny said the two most common problems pet owners had were aggression in dogs and soiling outside the litter box in cats. At that, I poised my pen over my notepad, hoping to get a free analysis of Goldie's peeing proclivities. I asked how they solved litter box rejection.

"There are two broad categories—is it preference or avoid-ance?" She then launched into such a lengthy description of the causes of cat elimination problems and the deductive skills needed to puzzle them out that I realized CBS could launch a new spinoff: *CSI: Cat Piss.*

By this time Quentin and his family had arrived. They went into a treatment room and I was put in the adjoining room, joined by several students, where I was able to watch the proceedings from behind a two-way mirror. It actually was like a TV crime series. Sitting in a semicircle was the family: mother, father, a daughter who looked about twenty and a son about sixteen. Three-year-old Quentin, looking unhappy and confused, was seated between the father's legs. His flat face was framed by big bat ears, and dominated by his huge, round eyes, one fireball red; he had a brindle coat and a white chest patch, a broad chest, and spindly legs. Since the French bulldog is one of the foundation breeds of the Boston terrier, my thigh started to throb while I was looking at Quentin. I was having a flashback to being attacked by Alastair.

The veterinarian, Dr. Ilana Reisner, walked in, along with Jenny, and a student. All three women took chairs set up at the farthest end of the room from Quentin. As soon as they entered Quentin stood at attention and began growling, low and deep, like the sound you hear near the San Andreas Fault just before things start shaking. The growling grew to a deafening, full-throated, teeth-baring bark. His red eye seemed lit with a Satanic fire and was focused directly on Dr. Reisner. Quentin strained at his leather leash as the father pulled it ever tighter. The father patted Quentin and murmured reassuringly to him, finally—suicidally, I thought—burying his face in Quentin's neck. Quentin quieted and sat back on his haunches. In looks and manner Quentin bore a remarkable resemblance to Stitch, the insane space creature in the Disney animated movie, who comes to earth and tries to pass as a dog.

"Why don't you tell us about Quentin's history," said Dr. Reisner with the calm tone of a dinner party hostess who was too polite to acknowledge that a drunken guest at the other end of the table had just dunked his feet into the soup.

The mother outlined Quentin's difficult life. He was living in deplorable conditions with a woman who had forty cats when the family adopted him as a puppy. All of his littermates had been poisoned; Quentin was the only survivor, and had stomach problems as a result. (This was sounding more and more like a detective series.) He also seemed to have hip abnormalities; his legs stiffened up after a walk. Then there was his eye. However, it was almost impossible to properly diagnose, let alone treat, any of these maladies because even with Quentin muzzled, no vet wanted to do a thorough examination.

The family had also hired three trainers. "All of them said they were afraid," said the daughter. "Two refused to be in the same room." Not surprisingly, the attempts at remote behavior modification failed.

The family realized the situation with Quentin was spiraling out of control the day the mother brought him into the front yard with her, and although it was mid-morning on a school day, out of nowhere an eight-year-old boy appeared. Quentin went nuts. "Kids seem to freak him out," the mother said. He ran over to the boy, snapping at him. "I called out, 'Don't move!' but the boy started to walk away," the mother continued. Although Quentin did not bite—so far he has never bitten anyone—he jumped on the boy and scratched his arm. The mother frantically called Quentin to her and he slunk over, his ears down. "He looked embarrassed," she said.

"The other people who freak him out are the McDonald's drive-through person, bank tellers, the gas station attendant, and my older son when he comes home from college," continued the mother. While Quentin paid no attention to the family's two fifteen-year-old cats, possibly because the cat population had to reach a threshold of more than forty before it seemed unusual to him, they had to quarantine Quentin from the other family dogs, a husky mix, a Labrador, and the seeing-eye puppies the daughter raised.

The father, who was retired on disability, clearly felt it was time someone stood up for this reprobate: "I'm home with him all day. He's a loving, playful dog."

The veterinary student had a question: "Did any of the trainers mention euthanizing him?"

At that Quentin, who had been almost dozing between the father's legs, jumped to all fours and directed all his straining, salivating fury at the student.

When that attack passed the daughter replied, "They didn't. We knew that was the last option. That's why we wanted to come here."

Dr. Reisner said that Quentin suffered from generalized anxiety that manifested itself in aggression. He had a lot of strikes against him. He was improperly socialized as a puppy, and he might have been bred specifically to be a fighter. "He's reactive, quick to startle, grumpy and defensive," she said. I suddenly had a pang of empathy: that's what I'm like in the morning before the first cup of coffee. She said that his physical problems might be compounding his emotional ones. She suggested they make back-to-back appointments at the hospital with an ophthalmologist and orthopedist, heavily sedating Quentin before the examinations.

Without comprehensive treatment he presented a serious liability problem to the family, she warned. He needed to be under their control at all times. "Neutral human things can be very provocative to a dog," she said. A visitor to their home who decided to cross her legs could drive Quentin berserk, the doctor said. "The lady whose son was scratched can sue you," the doctor went on. "You can lose your homeowner's insurance." She interrupted herself and addressed the mother: "You look unhappy." Dr. Reisner's remarks had caused the family members to start curling over in their seats; they now looked like four overcooked shrimp. "I'm just listening," the mother replied.

Also listening was Quentin, who was fixing his red eye on Dr. Reisner. "He's stiffening, his pupils are dilated, he's aroused," the doctor said. "He is staring very intently at my shoe." The doctor was wearing a pair of clogs. Quentin clearly liked a woman in heels, because he looked as if he was about to devour the offending shoe and its wearer. Quentin erupted again, and again the father soothed him with pats and kisses.

Now for the good news. Quentin would benefit from intensive behavior modification therapy conducted by the family, and a prescription for antidepressants. The drugs were not a cure, but could dampen his behavior, Dr. Reisner said. The daughter expressed concern about possible side effects and the mother worried that the pills could upset his sensitive stomach. Behind the glass window I started shouting, "Hijack a Prozac truck! Build a

Quonset hut in the backyard and fill it with Zoloft! You're worried about his little tummy? How about worrying that all your visitors will end up footless!"

Dr. Reisner's good news came with a dose of bad news, like finding out your symptoms aren't AIDS, just herpes. She said that at the end of the regimen of behavior and drug therapy, "You will have a dog who's worried and reactive for the next fifteen years. That's who he is. It's always dogs like Quentin who live a long, healthy life." The family laughed, a sad, deflated laugh.

At that Dr. Reisner left, and Jenny took over. She gave the family a twenty-page handout and started demonstrating the exercises. I got a copy of the handout. The goal of most exercises seemed to be to get the dog to stay seated no matter what was going on. Most exercises began by commanding the dog to "Sit." They were from the book *Clinical Behavioral Medicine for Small Animals* by veterinarian Karen L. Overall. I was struck by one to desensitize a dog who gets upset when visitors come to the door. It read, only in part:

> Sit for 15 seconds while you clap and hum
> Sit while you leave the dog's view, knock or ring the bell, say "hello," talk for ten seconds, and return
> Sit for 20 seconds while you hum
> Sit while you leave the dog's view, say "hello," invite the invisible person in, wait 5 seconds, and return
> Sit while you leave the dog's view, say "hello," talk as if to someone for 5 seconds, and return
> Sit for 5 seconds while you hum and clap
> Sit while you run around the dog
> Sit while you leave the room and knock or ring the bell for 5 seconds

Sit while you leave the room and talk to people that aren't
   there for 10 seconds
Sit for 15 seconds while you jog and clap

I could see how this was a failproof system. At the end of several months of answering the door when no one was there, jogging around your dog, humming and clapping, and carrying on
conversations with invisible people, you would be so mentally
destabilized that even if your dog remained nuts, you'd no longer
notice.

Back home, about a week after observing Quentin, my daughter
and I were walking from the subway when I noticed across the
street a woman walking a Boston terrier. A large Boston terrier
with a brindle coat. "I think that's Alastair," I said to my daughter.
   My daughter grabbed my arm. "Mom, stay on this side of the
street," she said. "You don't need to get any closer. Look, he sees
you and he's licking his lips."
   I had to know, so I called across to the woman, "Hi, is that
Alastair?"
   She stopped and looked at me suspiciously. "Yes, how do you
know?"
   "Alastair bit me," I said.
   She gave me a long look. "Are you Elaine?" she said.
   Either she had gotten my name confused or Alastair had also
bitten a woman named Elaine.
   "I'm Emily."
   The woman stopped and got down on her knees next to Alastair
and started stroking him. "Yes, Todd told me about you," she
said coldly. "He says you're very interested in Alastair."
   Well, excuse me for being interested in a creature who decided
my thigh muscle was a Happy Meal. Maybe she had just acted

like a weepy, apologetic owner during our previous phone call as a ploy to keep me from suing her.

My daughter grabbed my arm and pulled me along. I looked back to see Alastair's owner French-kissing him and probably whispering, "Good riddance to that horrible Elaine who made you bite her."

31

THE MAN WHO LOVED DOGS

Our Todd.

I tried to get Sasha to one of Todd's classes once or twice a month. I accepted that dog training was like attending Alcoholics Anonymous meetings: If you ever needed to go, you'd probably always need to go. But we hadn't been for several months because of a series of overbooked weekends, and I noticed that Sasha seemed to be backsliding: pulling more on the leash, refusing to sit on first command. She needed a Todd booster shot. I marked "Todd" on my calendar for the following Sunday morning.

That week BREW asked me to do some home-checks for them. My daughter, Sasha, and I visited two families. One was an older, childless couple who wanted a companion for their eight-year-old beagle. The other was a gay couple who lived in a breathtaking mansion in Georgetown. As I was given a tour I started thinking, Forget adopting a beagle, adopt me.

I approved them both. My standard was that if you wanted a used beagle, you were 99 percent of the way there. Absent a sign on the front door saying, TAXIDERMY—BEAGLES ARE OUR

SPECIALTY, I figured, let them adopt. I wrote down Todd's e-mail for both couples, pressed it into their hands, and said, "You need to contact this man."

On Thursday I got an e-mail from the woman from PALS who led the nursing home visits Sasha and I had done. The subject line was "Sad News." Oh, dear, I thought, her dog must have died. I opened the e-mail. A memorial service for Todd was being planned, I read. "He died last week by his own hand," the message said.

No, not *my* Todd. There must be some mistake. I clicked to his Web site. In large letters across the bottom were the words, "In Loving Memory—Todd we will miss you!" It gave the time and place for us to gather on Sunday to honor him. But, Todd, I'm going to your *class* on Sunday, I said to myself. I have you written in the calendar.

Crying, I called Todd's friend Susan, the woman who took photos at every class. My daughter and I were thrilled every time Sasha's picture got posted on his Web site.

Susan was crying, too. She told me Todd had been missing for the past several days. The police finally found him in his van; he had died of carbon monoxide poisoning. The unraveling started, she said, when he boarded the dog of a client who went on vacation. While they were gone the dog died. No one knew what happened—had one of the other dogs attacked it, had it run into the street? But clearly Todd was embarrassed and ashamed. He loved dogs so much and one had died on his watch. When the woman came to claim her dog, he told her it had died and he had buried it on farmland in the country. She demanded the body back, but a few days later he told her he couldn't find where he had buried the dog.

The woman, understandably, was enraged. She believed her dog might have gotten lost, or Todd might have sold it. She put out flyers about her dog. The police came to question Todd. County officials shut down his boarding business. Finally, a reporter from the *Washington Post* heard about the situation and interviewed Todd. The paper decided not to do a story, but Todd didn't know that. He left a message on his answering machine telling his clients he couldn't return any more calls, and ended with, "It's been fun. I love you all."

On Saturday morning I went to the pool hall where Todd's classes met. What if someone who didn't know the terrible news was there waiting with a dog? I also went because I still didn't believe it. I thought if Sasha and I came, I would see Todd marching down the street, leading his caravan of dogs. The sidewalk was empty.

There were about a hundred people and as many dogs at the memorial service, held in the backyard of one of Todd's clients. If it hadn't been so heartbreaking, it would have been wonderful. It looked like a page out of *Go, Dog. Go!*—beagles, corgis, Weimaraners, basset hounds, Labradors, Afghans, poodles, and mutts. All of them behaving themselves; they had been trained by Todd.

When I went to express my condolences to his beautiful, composed wife she said, "He was so strong. So proud. Like an oak tree. And he broke. He loved dogs. He loved dogs."

People took turns walking up to the microphone with their dogs to tell Todd stories.

One woman told of how Todd helped her through the death of her elderly dog. "Then I got a new dog, Rufus, and you told me I deserved him. Todd, your work wasn't done. Todd wanted us to have wonderful dogs and we do because of him."

"Todd and I shared being teachers," said another woman, who had a wonderfully behaved beagle, Harley, I knew from class. "Every Saturday and Sunday I looked forward to dog school. My family thought it was odd that I would go every week, in heat and cold, but Todd was like a magnet to me and the dogs. All the dogs I saw this week, I wondered if they were all grieving as we were."

As I listened, I was struck by something. I knew Todd had a lot of clients, but I always felt he and I had a special relationship, that we particularly hit it off, and that he took an unusual interest in Sasha. But all of Todd's clients felt that way; he had the gift of making everyone feel that way.

For months after Todd died I went to his Web site to look at the photographs and read the memorials people posted. On one page of the Web site were pictures of dogs Todd had trained. If you clicked through, there were little stories written by the owner. One was labeled "Champ" but had no photo. I clicked on it. It was a story by Todd, about his first dog. He described how when he was six his parents took him to a pet store and paid $5 for a little Lab mix Todd named Champ. "For the next few days I was with Champ twenty-four hours a day," he wrote. "I even slept in the bathroom tub to be near him while he slept on the floor (covered with newspapers). This was before crate training was ever heard of." Todd's grandfather was a horse trainer, and he imparted to Todd most of the animal training lessons that Todd later applied to dogs. For four years Champ walked with Todd to school, returned home by himself, then walked back to school at three P.M. to meet Todd at the end of the day.

"Then one Friday morning I noticed he was moving slowly and for the first time he didn't follow me to school," Todd wrote. "My parents and I took him to the vet . . . Champ had cancer in his neck and wouldn't make it. I couldn't imagine life without Champ. All my family came to the vet so that we could say goodbye to Champ. He died in my arms." Todd couldn't go to school on Monday, he was so distraught. Around noon his grandmother told him to go to his bedroom window. Outside was his entire class, most carrying flowers. They waved to Todd and laid the flowers next to Champ's doghouse. "For me, at that very moment in Oct. 1964, that was the moment that I personally learned just how important our pets were to us and our friends . . . I am a trainer because of him. 42 years later I think of him every day. Thank you Champ . . . I will always love what you did for me."

Thank you, Todd. I will always love what you did for Sasha. And for me.

32

HOW MUCH IS THAT DOGGY IN THE PIGPEN?

My sister becomes a dog owner, again.

My sister had accommodated herself to a life without dogs. She moved from Seattle to Los Angeles, got a new boyfriend and business partner, Tony, a documentary filmmaker. She tried to submerge her dog desire into the two abandoned cats she adopted. Liz and Tony were finishing one of their projects and Liz was barely sleeping or eating and frantically running around L.A. to get all the technical details finished.

As she was driving home mid-afternoon from a meeting, her left hand started shaking. She pulled over and called Tony. He picked her up and took her home. The shaking accelerated and they decided she should go to the hospital. On their way out the door Liz collapsed. She had two grand mal seizures. The neurologist who examined her said it was probably due to scar tissue from her stroke, thirteen years earlier, and that the stress and lack of food and sleep had weakened her.

"When she got sick I said, that's it, we've got to get out of L.A, and she needs a dog," said Tony.

They sold the condo and bought a house on five acres in Oroville, California, in the mountains where the Gold Rush started. Two months after they arrived there, my husband, daughter, and I visited them, and they told us about their attempts to get a dog.

All Liz's previous dogs had been from breeders, so she figured she would have better luck getting a mutt from a shelter. They agreed they didn't want to deal with a puppy, but were looking for a young dog. Tony made her promise she would have no part in the selection. "I can't pick animals. I attract disaster," she admitted.

There were two shelters in town; the closest was the country kill shelter. One day Tony and Liz drove over. Liz waited in the car while Tony went in. Somewhere in the shelter the pipes had sprung a leak. The floor was covered with filthy water and Tony sloshed around looking for an employee. Finally, he was greeted by a man with one violently bloodshot eye carrying a folded belt in his hand. He directed Tony to a huge woman with inch-thick pancake makeup who never made eye contact with Tony. She led him down a wet, dingy corridor. The first pen they passed contained a three-hundred-pound potbellied pig lying on a pillow being lapped by water. The next cage had a litter of German shepherd puppies. "The whole shelter was nothing but pigs and puppies," says Tony.

He walked to the next cage and it held five little Labrador mixes, four black and one chocolate. The five were falling all over each other playing, but when Tony stood in front of the cage the chocolate one detached himself from the group and sat in the front of the cage, staring at Tony. "It was like he was saying to me, 'I'm done playing, I'm ready to go home now.'"

Tony told the woman he wanted that dog. Because the dogs were found dumped by the side of the road the day before, the shelter was required to hold them for four more days in case the owner turned up. This was Friday, so the woman told him to be back Monday for the dog. "If you're not here Monday," she said ominously, "it will be too late."

The notice on the cage listed the dogs' ages as: "12–24." When Tony got back in the car he told Liz he had picked a chocolate Labrador mix that was one to two years old.

"Oh, I can't wait," Liz said. "How big is he?"

Tony indicated with his hands about the size of their toaster oven.

"Is he a miniature Lab?" Liz asked, not sure there was such a thing. "He should be full-grown by now."

Besides a dog to fulfill Liz's longing, they wanted one to guard the property. Tony started worrying that the little dog he'd just picked wouldn't be able to protect them. So they decided to get another dog, one with more heft. Off they went to the other shelter. They said they wanted a large, adult dog, and the employee took them to a black Lab mix who had been in the shelter a month. She too had been found wandering along the road. When she was discovered her nipples were hugely enlarged; she obviously had just had puppies, but the rescuer couldn't locate them.

The black Lab was just the right size. She sat and lay down for them. They walked her through the part of the shelter that housed the cats, and they didn't bother her. They took her and named her Clarity. She had just been spayed and still had her stitches in, so they set up a bed for her in a walk-in closet where she could recuperate.

Liz called the first shelter and asked what kind of food she should get for the small dog. "Puppy food," the woman said.

"Why?" Liz asked.

"Because your puppy is twelve weeks old," was the reply.

She turned to Tony. "The dog is twelve weeks, not twelve months. Congratulations, you have a baby."

Monday morning Tony and Liz went to get the puppy. They named him Kubrick, after the late film director Stanley Kubrick. Their Kubrick was sleeping alone, his four black brothers all dozing in a pile together. At the sound of Tony's footsteps Kubrick ran to the front of his cage and waited for it to be opened. Tony carried him to the car, feeling terrible about the littermates he was leaving behind. He handed Kubrick to Liz, and the puppy immediately fell asleep in her lap. She was in heaven.

Kubrick was a bouncy, happy puppy. They took him to the vet the next day for his shots. "You've got a winner here. He's healthy, and he's going to be big," the vet said. They thought as much; the little dog had paws the size of cupcakes. Kubrick got his shots, a deworming medication, and a dose of flea repellent on his skin.

The next morning when they took him out for his walk, they noticed his poop was full of worms. Then he started throwing up. He threw up so much that finally only bile came out. When they took him for a walk later in the day, he had blood-filled diarrhea. They drove back to the vet, who was horrified.

The vet didn't know what was wrong, but he gave Kubrick a prescription for antibiotics and told them to keep their eye on him. He seemed to improve for a day, though he wouldn't eat. The next night he started pumping out vomit and they drove him to the emergency animal hospital. No one there could figure out what was wrong, either, but they put him on intravenous antibiotics and fluids. The emergency hospital opened at seven P.M. and closed early in the morning, so Liz and Tony arrived first thing to have a look at their puppy.

There was no diagnosis, but the words "distemper" and "parvo" were mentioned. These are two deadly dog viruses. Kubrick had just been vaccinated for both so there was no way now to test and see if he had either disease—the vaccination meant he would be positive for antibodies. If it was distemper, and he lived, he would probably have lifelong seizures. Liz thought, I have seizures, I can't possibly have a dog with seizures. The vet said that with either virus there was a chance, a small one, Kubrick would pull through.

He was in no shape to go home, so Liz and Tony transported him the twenty-five miles across town to their regular vet. Liz asked if it would help if they found out if any of his littermates had come down with something. The doctor said it would. So Liz and Tony left Kubrick at the vet's office for the day, went home and called the shelter. They explained why they needed to know about the other Lab pups. The woman who answered put them on hold to look them up. She got back on the line and said, "It's too late." All the others had been put down. If they hadn't adopted Kubrick, he would already be dead. Now it was likely he was going to die anyway, and they'd only had him as a healthy dog for one day.

That night they went to pick up Kubrick when the vet's office closed to take him back to the emergency hospital. They knew his only hope of pulling through was to get twenty-four-hour medical care. On the long drive back to the emergency vet, they kept saying, "Kubie, don't join your brothers. Stay with us."

In the meantime, Clarity was healing from her spaying, but Liz and Tony were spending so much time shuttling back and forth between the doctors' offices that they had to leave Clarity in the house for long stretches. As a result she started peeing and pooping in the closet. Liz came home one day and looked at the condition of the closet, and thought of Kubrick's condition. She had the terrible feeling that even though she nobly spent years caring for Knut and Paris, she was being punished on some cosmic canine level with a set of two new dog catastrophes.

There was no treatment for either virus; the only hope was to keep Kubrick alive long enough for his immune system to kick in. Because Kubrick wouldn't eat or drink, the daytime vet injected fluids under Kubrick's skin to help keep him hydrated. He looked like a baby camel. On the drive back to the evening hospital, Liz massaged his hump and murmured encouragement to him.

One day when Tony was carrying Kubrick out of the vet's office he walked by a gardener, a grizzled older man working on the grounds. "You got a sick puppy?" the gardener mumbled.

"Yes, I do," replied Tony.

"That's parvo," the gardener said as he attacked the hedges with a pair of clippers. "They all got parvo. It's killing all the dogs of Oroville." Tony felt like he'd had an encounter with a gardener from a Stephen King novel.

By the fifth day, when they arrived at either office, the vet techs would start crying at the sight of Kubrick. Everyone was getting so attached to him. They told Liz and Tony that the dog would surely be dead if not for their commitment. They marveled that the couple would do this for a puppy they'd only had for a day.

On the sixth day Kubrick still hadn't eaten. When they brought him back to the day vet, after he had been put in the cage, Liz stuck her finger in a bowl of gruel and brought it to Kubrick's mouth. He licked it. She was so happy, until he fell into a spasm of mucus-filled coughing. Later that morning the tech called with good news and bad news. The good news was that Kubrick ate and drank. The bad news was that immediately afterward he had explosive diarrhea all over his cage. The next day his temperature shot up to 106.

Liz and Tony said maybe they needed to let go. Maybe Kubrick did indeed want to be with his brothers. But almost immediately he started to get better. After eight days in two hospitals, and a bill totaling $2,000, they took their puppy back home. In his three months on earth he had cheated death three times: once when he was rescued, once when he was adopted, and once when he survived a deadly virus.

For a few days while he regained his strength they kept him apart from Clarity, who was now fully recovered and learning to go in the yard. Then the big moment came, and they allowed the two dogs to meet. Liz and Tony hovered over them, worried that Clarity might attack the puppy.

When they saw each other they started a ballet, twirling and jumping around each other for joy. They spun in the air, Clarity sniffed Kubrick, they rolled on the ground, Clarity let Kubrick playfully bite her. Then Kubrick tried to nurse on Clarity. Liz and Tony looked at each other. Clarity was a black Lab mix who had just had puppies and been found wandering in Oroville. Kubrick was a chocolate Lab mix, the only brown puppy in a litter of black, who had been found abandoned in Oroville.

"I think she might be his mother," Liz said to Tony.

"I think she is his mother," my daughter said upon hearing this part of the story. "Look, they have the same eyes."

Both dogs, who were playing in the living room, Kubrick still awkward on his outsized puppy paws, looked at us at that moment. She was right, they did.

33

CRAZY THEY CALL ME

We look for another dog.

I was so far gone that I was starting to think about getting another dog. We were set up for it, we had the fence, the crates, the food. I was already a prisoner in my own home, so why not get a companion for Sasha? Why not have a dog like Roscoe, who would comfort my husband by dozing with its snout in his armpit? I had fantasies of pulling weeds in the front yard, or reading on the porch, accompanied by an adorable mutt who didn't need a leash and was happy just to hang around me.

When I thought about what kind of dog I wanted I kept coming back to a scene from the recent Beaglefest we'd attended. Beaglefest is BREW's annual fund-raising event, a chance for BREW adopters to swap stories and their dogs to swap scent gland aromas. The conversation there made me think of a parole officer's convention—everyone was subtly competing to show they had been able to turn around the most hard-core cases. Beaglefest was held at a dog-boarding facility, so there was a secure, fenced area large enough for a hundred milling beagles. Getting past the double row of fencing guarded by human monitors was like passing through the airlock system at a biosafety level one containment facility.

A woman sat on the ground with her young children and a huge beagle who seemed oblivious to the frenzy. The beagle had striking coloring, it was almost completely white, as if it had been bleached from being left in the sun too long. It turned out it was a grizzled, white-muzzled twelve-year-old. The woman said they had adopted it at age eight, and because it was so mellow it was perfect for toddlers. I thought there was a certain genius to this. A geriatric dog will put up with your toddlers' abuse, and won't hang around long enough so that you are still walking it after the kids depart for college.

I decided we would find the Grandma Moses of dogs—something spry with late-blooming talents. We would have a wonderful few years, then it would thoughtfully drop dead. (More likely, I would end up with an impossibly decrepit, failing dog, and I wouldn't be able to let go.)

I went back to the unwanted-dog Web sites. At petfinders.com I couldn't help myself and under "breed" I typed in "Boston terrier." It turns out you can search all of North America and not find an old, well-mannered Boston terrier who gets along with kids, cats, and other dogs. The only possibility was a mix that looked suspiciously pit bullish. My daughter came in and I showed her.

"Mom, no! Look at that dog, Mom. Can't you tell that dog wants to bite you!" We kept scrolling.

My daughter wrote down the small list of possibilities. One was a border collie. His name was Simon and he had beautiful blue eyes. However, his foster mother said he could not be taken off his leash. I liked a regular collie with a sweet face and a naked body—he'd been shaved for reasons understandably unspecified in his ad. My husband recoiled.

It was time to go back to the shelters. When you say to the volunteers, "I'm looking for a really old dog," they give you a slightly suspicious look. What did they think, we wanted the old mutt's pension? I explained that we wanted to be—in dog-rescue nomenclature—a "forever family," we just didn't want to be one forever.

We toured the cages reading the estimated ages. A volunteer said there were a bunch of old, small dogs boarding in the cat room. We saw a Chihuahua, a shih tzu, and a Lhasa apso. They were old, all right. They were also crusty and comatose. There were no appealing, medium-sized, old dogs. But my husband was drawn to a scrawny border collie when their eyes met and the dog locked onto him.

There is something uncanny about border collies. I'm not even sure they are dogs, but perhaps some new species on the borderline between canine and human—border sapiens. That, at least, is what a recent study of a German border collie, Rico, would indicate. He made worldwide headlines when it was revealed that not only could he understand more than two hundred words, he could deduce the meaning of new ones.

In our own neighborhood we had dealt with the problem that border collies make you feel like your dog has the intelligence of the fungus that causes jock itch. Around the corner from us lived one who, each time you passed by its house, would knock with its nose a perfectly timed tennis ball to your feet. You simply had to stop and play.

With the arrival of Sasha we actually talked to the owner of the ball-playing dog—naturally only exchanging dog, not human, names. Oh, cruel irony, the border collie's name was Sasha. We took to referring to her as "Sasha the Wonder Dog." It was painful to walk by her house and have our Sasha bark like a maniac at Sasha TWD, while Sasha TWD calmly nosed balls our way. Once Sasha TWD and her owner turned up our block—Sasha

TWD of course needed no leash—just as my daughter and I were taking Sasha for a walk. I said to my daughter, "Look, it's Sasha the Wonder Dog!" The owner looked perplexed, and I explained that our Sasha didn't have quite the range of skills her Sasha possessed.

"I'm sure that your Sasha is the most intelligent, loving dog in the world," she said with a mixture of kindness and condescension. It must have been the same tone Mrs. Einstein used when she said, "Your child must be very bright, too."

At the shelter, my husband kept calling us over to observe the amazing border collie. "Watch, whatever I do, she can't take her eyes off me." We were dissuaded from adopting our own wonder dog when the shelter volunteer explained this one was hostile to other dogs.

Then, late one night, scrolling the Web, I saw the elderly dog I knew was meant for us. Although we didn't want a big dog, the description said she was an old German shepherd–Labrador retriever mix who weighed about eighty pounds. "I get along well with adults, kids, other dogs, cats," the ad read. Her name was Brandy. A German shepherd named Brandy! In some grand karmic way I could give the love to this Brandy that I had withheld from my childhood Brandy.

I showed Brandy's picture to my husband. "She's awfully big," he said.

"Her name is *Brandy*," I said. He agreed I could check her out.

I called the county shelter and they referred me to a veterinarian who was fostering Brandy. The vet said Brandy was about ten years old and her owner had given her up because she ran away and also because he decided she had a huge tumor in her abdomen, which turned out to be a fatty deposit. Since my abdomen also has a fatty deposit, we obviously belonged together. The vet said she was gentle and mellow, but despite her listing, the vet didn't know how Brandy would do with cats. She suggested I try her out for the weekend, but first I needed to get permission from the county animal officer.

I called the officer and explained why I was interested in Brandy—that I particularly wanted a dog who could safely be taken off-leash.

"Brandy can't be taken off-leash," she said. "She's an explorer and she's not car smart. With her previous owners she would jump the fence and get out. She was going to get killed." I was crushed. I would have to undo my Brandy karma some other way.

Shortly afterward I found another German shepherd, Gretchen, who sounded perfect—loyal, friendly, smart, obedient, good with kids, cats, dogs. Her owner had given her up when she (the owner) became pregnant. I e-mailed and expressed my interest. I got a quick e-mail back saying that Gretchen truly was as described, so much so that her foster mother had decided to adopt her.

I know my next dog is out there waiting for me to claim it (so it can immediately become incontinent). We will find each other. After all, I did inherit the dog person gene.

34

"SASHA, NO!"

A beagle can never be let off-leash.

Then, what I'd been dreading happened.

Spring had arrived and with the longer evenings our neighborhood of semidetached houses became one big playground. Love was also in the air—young, doomed love.

The five-year-old boy across the street, Micah, developed a sudden, intense passion for my eight-year-old daughter. He followed her moonily as she played with the other kids. He tried to horn in on private get-togethers she had with her seven-year-old best friend on the block. He boldly rang the bell and asked if she could play. Once, when a group of kids was outside he said to my daughter, "It's been so long since I've been in your house, I can't even remember what it looks like. Maybe you should take me in so I can see it."

One evening after my daughter had indulgently played with Micah in a neighbor's backyard for about fifteen minutes, she came to the sidewalk where I had taken a break from walking Sasha to talk to the other parents. She whispered, "Mom, Micah is really bothering me and Catherine. He's following us everywhere." By that time he had trotted around to look at his beloved. "Why'd you stop playing?" he asked my daughter.

I had to act. "Micah, do you think you could help me walk Sasha?"

"What a great idea!" his mother chimed in, seeing that her son's romance was heading toward the shoals.

Before he could object, his mother nudged him to me. I had him grasp Sasha's leash halfway down its length, while I held on to the end. He gave her a backward jerk. "Micah, don't yank on her, let her walk and she'll pull you along," I said.

"I want to hold her myself. I can do it," he insisted.

I hesitated. His mother said, "Micah, if you walk her, you have to hold her with two hands." He put both hands on the leash; I hovered. The street was quiet, and Micah got pulled along by Sasha for a few seconds.

Then, on the other side of the street, turning a corner, were a woman and a large, curly-haired dog. Sasha saw them immediately, and slipped out of Micah's hands like a marlin on the end of a fishing pole.

In a perfect, sickening piece of choreography, as Sasha bolted into the street, a car turned the corner. I screamed, "Sasha, NO!" It was too late. Sasha was halfway across just as the car intersected her path. I heard the thump and watched her roll under the wheels, blood staining her fur. I was sure I had just witnessed the death of my dog.

My husband and I had talked about this moment. In recent months, Sasha's desire to run free had escalated. She lurked around the door whenever we were going out. Several times, despite our shooing her away, she managed to squeeze through a crack in the storm door and dash into the street. We put a bottle of bitter apple spray in the foyer and dosed her when she got too close to freedom, trying to break her of this life-threatening habit.

And now she was under a car and it was my fault. The driver had excellent reflexes and stopped immediately. When she did, Sasha tried to right herself. She was alive! The driver, a young woman dressed in hospital scrubs, got out of the car and stood, looking stricken at the carnage. The owner of the other dog was crying and calling out, "I'm so sorry, I'm so sorry." I picked up Sasha. I called to the driver and the dog owner, "It's not your fault!" and ran home with her to get my purse and the car keys. She was alert but damaged. I could feel her blood spurting down my pants. Her left rear leg looked like a fur coat that had been slashed to the lining.

I had a neighbor get my daughter from her friend's house. I needed her to keep Sasha still in the backseat. My daughter was shaken but remained calm. But when I asked her to pat Sasha she said, "Mom, I can see her bone. I can't look at her." Although our veterinarian's office is famous for its high fees, it is five minutes from my house, open twenty-four hours a day, and full of well-trained professionals. The technician took Sasha to the back and my daughter and I waited. Once the receptionist saw the condition of my pants, she gently suggested we go to a private room.

"I remember when Dad told me how Grandma told him that his dog had been hit by a car and died. He said he had a lump in his throat, and now I know what he means," my daughter said. "My body is telling me I should cry, but I just don't want to."

I told her that I felt like crying, too, but I also didn't want to. And that maybe we weren't crying because it looked like Sasha might be all right.

The doctor came out. She was young and pretty, and exuded competence. She gave us a tutorial in crush injuries, shearing wounds, ligament dissections, internal organ trauma, the function of the tibia and fibula. In the end, she said Sasha was mightily bruised, and her leg was badly torn up, but she was probably going to make it. The doctor said she was eager to get in and try to sew the severed ligaments together, but she would decide in a few hours whether to operate.

I asked the doctor whether Sasha would be more car savvy after this.

"No," she said. "She's a beagle." She told us that her parents got their beagle when it was hit by a car in front of their house and the owner didn't want to pay the hospital bill. That beagle hadn't learned anything about cars, either.

Then she cleared her throat and dropped her voice, as if imparting classified information. "This is going to be expensive," she said. She started ticking off charges: X rays, surgery, antibiotics, hospitalization. "I know," I said. "I know. Just do what you have to do." I left a deposit for $1,000.

While we waited for the results from the X rays, I thought about Micah. I had lost track of him in all the confusion. I didn't get to tell him, too, that it wasn't his fault. I was so worried he would not only be traumatized by the events, but would think he was responsible for hurting the dog of his beloved. My daughter and I agreed that when we got home we would take a little present to him and a card.

When we returned, there was a note in the mailbox from Micah, written by his mother. "Dear Sasha, I'm worried about you. If you need a bandage, I can give you one. If you need a doggy treat, I can bring you one. I hope you are better soon."

Before I cleaned the blood out of the car, I helped my daughter put together a gift bag, and she delivered it. The sight of my daughter and the news that Sasha was alive transformed Micah into a happy boy again, his mother whispered to me.

I scrubbed out the car and washed my clothes. Every couple of hours an internal clock jolted me with a reminder, "Time to take Sasha out." Her absence made me see how thoroughly she had insinuated herself into my unconscious. Checking on her whereabouts and her needs were part of the rhythm of my life. At about ten-thirty the doctor called back and said she wanted to put off the operation until the morning. "I really want to fix it. But she got such a wallop, I just have a gut feeling it would be better to wait. She's stable, but I've seen enough times where they look stable and they die under anesthesia." Go with your gut, Doc!

It was lonely in the morning without Sasha hovering for crumbs from our breakfast cereal. I called the hospital at eleven A.M. Another surgeon had just finished Sasha's leg. She told me that she could only find one end of her ligament, so she patched her back together as best she could. We had two choices. We could take her home that night with a splint and see how she healed over the next two months. Or, for about $1,500 more we could have an orthopedist go in and make a more sophisticated repair of her leg. If she healed all right without the second surgery, she might have a little limp.

I e-mailed my dog-crazy sister and asked what she'd do. She wrote back: "Personally, I don't think there's anything wrong with having a limp. I think it's rather charming. Seriously, if she can function fine without the surgery it's no big deal." I hadn't even been thinking about my sister's residual limp from her stroke. I also talked with a friend who was an emergency room doctor and dog lover. She said to wait and see how the leg healed.

We brought Sasha home that night. She was woozy and had a bright pink bandage wrapped around the splint on her leg. My instructions were to keep her off her feet, and carry her outside when she had to go. She reminded me of when we first got her: sweet, confused, and scared. Only now she was reassured by my presence and I was reassured by hers. As I held her in my arms, she licked me, and pressed her head against my elbow. "I'm so glad you made it, little one," I said. She let out a deep sigh.

By the following week, Sasha was perky again, and frustrated with her splinted leg and the lampshade collar she had to wear to keep her from shredding her bandage. My daughter's most dog-loving friend, Helen, came by to cheer up the patient. Sasha was thrilled for the company, jumping all over and licking Helen. Helen asked me to describe exactly how the accident happened.

"Sasha, I hope you've learned your lesson about cars," Helen said while looking into Sasha's face.

"Helen, I'm not sure Sasha is capable of learning that lesson," I said.

"Well, that's not something to be ashamed of, but it is something to work on," she replied. Amen.

After so many days of restricted activity, Sasha was desperate to get out of the house. My daughter and I took her for a little walk so she could relieve herself. I carried her down the stairs, and when I put her on the sidewalk she pulled up her left rear leg like a 727 retracting a landing gear, and took off. I had to pull on her leash to keep her from sprinting down the block. The first people we ran into were Micah and his family.

"She looks great! This is a miracle," his mother said. "I was so sure I saw this dog get killed last week. Killed. I'm still having flashbacks."

Micah was completely discombobulated by the joint appearance of my daughter and Sasha. But his twenty-month-old sister, an incipient dog person, ran over and embraced Sasha. "Good goggie! Good goggie!" Sasha endured her loving for a few minutes, but I could see she was desperate to get going. Her mother removed her from Sasha's back, and my daughter, Sasha, and I continued down the street.

After a few sadly comical crash landings of her plastic cone against the sidewalk as Sasha tried to sniff, she figured out how to maneuver it into the grass. It even seemed to help concentrate the aromas other dogs had left behind—she looked like a sommelier appreciating a fine vintage. Then she picked up her head and pulled us along. We were grateful she had miles of sniffing ahead of her.

DOG RESOURCES

You can't have Sasha—no matter what she does, we're keeping her. But you can rescue another wonderful dog from dire circumstances. The most obvious place to start is your local humane society, which is probably listed in your Yellow Pages under "animal shelter" or "humane societies." The Internet is also a great place to look for abandoned dogs. For example, www.pets911.com and www.petfinder.com will connect you to dozens of rescue groups, and the technology allows you to do everything from look at pictures of available mutts in your area to survey the nation for salukis, Samoyeds, or schipperkes. Do remember that when you read each dog's glowing recommendation, it was written by a dogist like me.

If you are interested in a beagle (if you are, perhaps you didn't read this book, but just skipped ahead to this page), and you live in the mid-Atlantic or Midwest, then tell www.brewbeagles.org that I sent you.

ACKNOWLEDGMENTS

This book started with an article on Slate.com, where I have been able to write about such things as my animals' bodily functions while my brilliant colleagues write about how to save the world. Thanks especially to founding editor Michael Kinsley, editor Jacob Weisberg, and deputy editor David Plotz, who have always made my work better.

I met Mimi Swartz two decades ago at *Texas Monthly*. Since then, I have relied on her journalistic judgment and her friendship. Thanks to my wonderful agent, David McCormick, who made this book possible. It has been a privilege to work with two superb editors at Bloomsbury, Colin Dickerman and Kathy Belden. Oh, how they improved this book.

So many family members, friends, and friends of friends have shared their dog stories with me. I will be forever grateful for their patience and generosity, and for the heroics and nuttiness of their dogs. Thanks to the volunteers of Beagle Rescue Education and Welfare, who have saved thousands of dogs and who thought one shaky little one would be right for us.

Most of all I want to thank my husband and daughter. They made me get Sasha; they allowed me to quote them; they bring me more happiness than I ever thought possible.

A NOTE ON THE AUTHOR

Emily Yoffe is a contributing writer to Slate.com and a widely published journalist. She has written for *Esquire, Health,* the *Los Angeles Times,* the *New York Times, O Magazine,* and *Texas Monthly,* among many others. She lives in Washington, D.C., with her husband and daughter, their two cats, and their beagle Sasha.

A NOTE ON THE TYPE

The text of this book is set in Linotype Sabon, named after the type founder Jacques Sabon. It was designed by Jan Tschichold and jointly developed by Linotype, Monotype, and Stempel, in response to a need for a typeface to be available in identical form for mechanical hot metal composition and hand composition using foundry type. Tschichold based his design for Sabon roman on a font engraved by Garamond, and Sabon italic on a font by Granjon. It was first used in 1966 and has proved an enduring modern classic.